Life in
THE VILLA
IN ROMAN BRITAIN

Life in

THE VILLA
IN ROMAN BRITAIN

JOHN BURKE

B.T. Batsford Ltd, *London*

First published 1978
© John Burke 1978
ISBN 0 7134 1013 2

Filmset in 'Monophoto' Garamond by
Servis Filmsetting Ltd, Manchester

Printed in Great Britain by
Cox & Wyman Ltd, Fakenham
for the publishers B.T. Batsford Ltd
4 Fitzhardinge Street, London W1H 0AH

CONTENTS

ACKNOWLEDGMENTS

The Author and Publisher would particularly like to thank Marian Berman for her picture research and the following for the illustrations which appear in this book:

Colchester and Essex Museum 1, 44; Landesmuseum, Trier 3, 15, 37b; Photo Aerofilms 4, 11, 43; Society of Antiquaries of London 5; Gloucester City and Folk Museums 6; Crown Copyright. Reproduced with permission of H.M. Stationery Office 7, 33, 62, 67, 74; Trustees of the British Museum 8, 26, 27, 30, 37d, 37e, 37g, 38, 42, 48, 50, 51, 52e, 56, 63, 66, 68, 75, 78; University of Cambridge, Crown Copyright Reserved 9; Chester Museum 10; Oliver Cook/Edwin Smith 12a; Sussex Archaeological Society 12b; Ashmoleon Museum, Oxford 14, 55; A. F. Kersting 23, 60, 70, 79; Sussex Archaeological Trust 25, 28, 61; Estate of Alan Sorrell 29, 73; National Monuments Record, Crown Copyright 2, 21a, 39; Warburg Institute 3, 16, 47; Verulamium Museum 32; Kölnisches Stadtmuseum 34; City and Council Museum, Lincoln 36; Museum of London 37a, 37f, 41, 46, 54, 65; National Museum of Antiquities of London 37c; Trustees of Collection (Chesters Museum) and the University Library, Newcastle-upon-Tyne 40; Musée Gaumais, Virton, Belgium 49; National Museum of Antiquities of Scotland 52a–c, 77; Reading Museum 52d, 53b; Bards Museum 53a; Thames and Hudson Ltd 53c; Bath City Council 71, 72; Hull Museum 80.

LIST OF ILLUSTRATIONS

8

INTRODUCTION

Although the Romans were assiduous chroniclers of their military triumphs and the achievements and failings of their various generals, Caesars and Emperors, they have left few written references to domestic life in Britain during its centuries as a Roman province. Pliny the Younger and other letter-writers and poets provide us with descriptions, sometimes rather literary and affected, of their villas and life in the countryside: but it is the Continental countryside. No educated Romano–Briton seems to have had any urge to record his experiences and observations for posterity. There are no Paston Letters, no colourful memoirs such as those of Peninsular or First World War infantrymen; no Kilvert's Diary, and no Celia Fiennes or William Cobbett riding inquisitively about the land.

Some people and their doings are, it is true, commemorated in stone, and here we do receive a little help. The Romans were as earnest in the recording of facts and dates on their edifices as a modern mayor or county councillor is in immortalising his name on the foundation stone of a new town hall. From milestones, the plinths of statues, and the façades of buildings sacred and secular we can learn something at least of the development of towns, temples and thoroughfares. Perhaps beginning with a dedication to a god, or going straight into a carved recital of the titles and virtues of the current Emperor, such inscriptions would go on to name the builder, to state whether the building is a new one or perhaps the reconstruction of some earlier gate or fortification, and in the case of some major work would often end with the identification of the legionary centuries – detachments of a hundred men under a centurion – which had done the hard manual labour.

On tombstones there are to be found more personal recollections, though usually phrased in such formal terms that they do little to bring the deceased or his background to life again. Only occasionally is there a flicker of something touching and human, as in a family scene on a stone coffin, or the discovery of toys in a child's grave.

In attempting a reconstruction of this vanished society we have to fit together a number of scattered shards which reappear on the surface of our modern world from time to time. A farmer's plough strikes a buried treasure; excavation for the foundations of a new office block reveals the

12

1
Tombstone of Marcus Favonius
Facilis, a centurion of the
Twentieth Legion at
Camulodunum (Colchester).
The finely executed details of
his uniform are remarkably
well preserved, including the
vitis or vine staff as symbol of
his rank, and there are
indications that the figure may
originally have been brightly
painted.

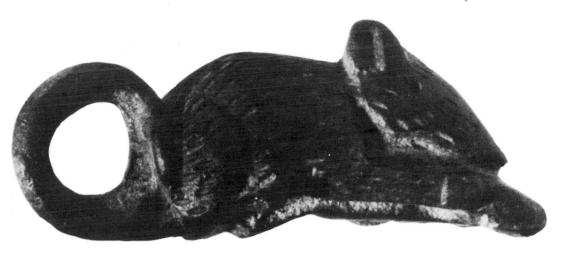

earlier foundations of a Roman fort; a fence post driven into the ground encounters a tile or the corner of a mosaic floor several inches down, and with infinite patience the outlines of a house can be brought back into the light.

But how did the possessors of that treasure, the garrison of that sort, or the family of the richly decorated villa, live? What clothes or uniform did they wear, what games occupied their leisure hours, what feasts or snacks did they have?

Evidence from archaeological excavations helps to fill in some of the gaps, but still we do not, as it were, hear the authentic voices of the people themselves. At best we can compare ruins and relics in this country with those in other parts of what was once the Roman Empire, and cautiously interpret for our own context the more substantial written records of Roman parallels. A villa in Dorset may not be an identical copy of a villa in Tuscany, but because Roman ideas and standards were applied as nearly consistently as possible throughout the Empire, with tactful or slyly subversive adaptations to certain ineradicable local usages, it is reasonable to draw conclusions from the one which will relate to the other. Some crops in Spain, Gaul or Calabria would not be found in the different soils and climate of Britain, and there would be differences in the national temperaments of both owner and labourer. At the same time, some influences carried by Roman administrators and settlers into the island province would take root and help to fashion methods of working and ways of living.

In putting the picture together it is risky to read into it too many present-day parallels, or indeed to force the pieces of the jigsaw into a distorted shape in order to create parallels where none really exist. We should not seek to visualise a Romano–British villa's absentee landlord in exactly the same rôle as a tax-loss farmer of our own time, or dream up modern viewpoints and dialogue for family and servants in the style of so many pseudo-historical novels and plays. Nevertheless history would be a dull subject if it merely listed names, dates, and pedantically verifiable facts. Excavated relics plus heaps of collapsed stone plus inscriptions plus documents plus imagination should at least open up a window on to a not too incredible, not too blurred scene – provided the imagination is not allowed *too* much freedom. Even if one guesses some of the answers wrong, it is impossible for an inquiring mind not to ask the questions in the first place, and not to indulge in reasonable speculation.

If in the pages which follow there are times when the reader feels that dramatic enthusiasm has carried the author away, I apologise; but I do not think I have taken too many outrageous liberties in the assembly and interpretation of facts and possibilities.

CHAPTER I

TOWN
& COUNTRY

The collector of port dues and taxes must have had many a trying week, when all that kept him going was the thought of his weekend in the country and the promise of eventual retirement there. In his office near the quayside he was beset from all sides by dishonesty and incompetence. Merchants tried to falsify their manifests; important military cargoes went astray or arrived late; his procurator was often in a bad mood because of harassment from the imperial legate in his palace on the outskirts of the city; and that mood became worse when the legate himself, reprimanded in despatches from Rome for certain omissions and a tendency to take his comforts too much for granted, took out his anger on his subordinates.

In spite of the inadvisability of drawing too many parallels, we do seem to be talking of someone not unlike a modern civil servant waiting for the moment on Friday afternoon when he can slip away to his car and drive out to that riverside or seaside cottage to which one day he will eventually move for good and there cultivate a patch of garden; but in this case the civil servant is Romano–British. He had a town house and a town office, and had worked hard and saved hard to buy himself a country estate. Like his twentieth-century counterpart, he doubtless devoted his spare moments to thoughts of the improvements he wanted to make to his villa, to plans for developing land so far untilled or not providing an adequate yield, and to the cost of installing a new bath-house.

One of his troubles would have been, as it is for the modern owner of a second house far from the city, that in order to maintain it in his own absence and prepare it for his full-time residence in due course, he needed to hold down his present job and work hard for increases in salary.

Furthermore, the tax system in which he himself played an administrative part demanded that country estates should yield profit in the form of food-stuffs for the cities and above all for the military. A country villa was not merely an isolated holiday retreat: it had to be the centre of a working community. Many such began as the home farms of small agricultural estates and grew as the owners prospered; or perhaps were taken over by richer neighbours or by city officials with ambitions to become gentlemen farmers. A resident landlord might already have one sumptuous villa for himself and

3
A wall painting from Trier depicting a corridor villa with corner towers.

find it convenient to purchase a smaller adjacent property and convert it into a home for his bailiff, together with outbuildings used as stores or slave quarters. An absentee landlord hoped to improve on his initial investment and secure his future in retirement; but until that day would have the additional expense of installing this resident *vilicus*, or bailiff, who would be allowed considerable freedom in the day-to-day, season-to-season running of the farm.

Our city official has chosen his site with care. Naturally the house and lands must be reasonably near a good road, both for ease of transport of produce to market and to expedite his own trips to his property. A good water supply is essential. What better, then, than an estate not too far beyond the foothills of the littoral, with a stream from which domestic supplies can be taken, and meadows irrigated by the waters of the lower downlands? On all sides the prospect is pleasing. Thick forest halts a couple of miles to the east, where the first settlers hacked out extensive clearings, and rings one re-assuringly round to the north. Through the trees and over the hill cuts that confident military road which now sounds less frequently to the tramp of marching feet. Peace was established in these lowlands many years ago. Violence in the north means that a standing army must still be maintained in the province – and the province must pay for it – but the defending legionaries, like the barbarians, are largely out of sight, far away in the inhospitable hills.

Barbarian: strange that one's own ancestors should have been regarded by the Roman invaders as barbarians; and strange how smoothly and swiftly a change of attitude was effected!

The Romans may be exasperating in their imperialist arrogance, in the meticulous detail of their administration from afar, and the subjugation of all other beliefs to their own concept of the state and its functions; but it has to be admitted that, once victorious, they have not merely treated the native Britons tolerantly but have actively encouraged them to take part in the civil administration and provided tempting patterns for their social ambitions. It surely makes sense to accept Roman dominance and Roman fashions if with them go such comforts as centrally-heated houses and villas and, at whatever cost in taxation, a reliable military defence force to ensure that no rival tribesmen will tear down your walls and slaughter your children. Better the food and wine and warmth and security of the Empire than the bleakness of those abandoned hill-top forts on the ridge above your placid pastures. Today those ramparts are no more than a memorial to olden times. The Romans have no practical use for them; and the new Romano–Britons have learned new ways.

*   *   *

The Celts whom Julius Caesar set out to subdue were not quite the ravening brutes he portrayed in parts of his account of the campaign. As Sir Mortimer Wheeler once commented, any general whose troops are set upon by a horde of enemy warriors out to kill will tend to regard the attackers as hideous and subnormal. One's own side is always the civilised, civilising one. The various tribes which made up Britain included, in fact, many enlightened (if minor) chieftains, a well-organised tribal aristocracy, and numbers of skilled craftsmen whose surviving work reveals fine creative imagination and taste.

They were practical men, too. The Belgae had transformed agriculture in northern Europe with their heavy ploughs, and after invading Britain set them to work here also. The plough hitherto used by the Iron Age Celts had been a primitive wooden share with a pointed iron tip. Enlarged by the Belgae with a longer and broader share, it became even more effective on heavy soils with the addition of a coulter to slice into the soil ahead of the share, and led to the exploitation of larger tracts of land than the characteristic small, square 'Celtic fields' with their lynchet embankments. Grain was dried in kilns and then stored in pits in the ground. Belgic methods were so successful that within a short time of their settlement they were actually exporting corn from their British fields across the Channel.

The Cornish tin trade had flourished for some centuries BC, and other exports included gold, silver, iron – and slaves, presumably taken in inter-tribal warfare.

Possibly the chance of bringing such resources exclusively under imperial control would sooner or later have tempted the Romans to invade the island. But their first assault might not have come when it did if the Belgae settled in Britain had not unwisely given succour to their kinsmen in Gaul and openly encouraged their defiance of Julius Caesar.

Caesar led punitive expeditions in 55 and 54 BC which did not penetrate far into the country, and made no attempt to bring the northern regions to heel. In his second attempt he succeeded, however, in defeating the most powerful alliances of the south. The principal chieftain, Cassivellaunus, surrendered. From him and the other more warlike elements Caesar extracted a promise of regular tribute to Rome and also an assurance that they would cease persecuting the less belligerent neighbouring tribes. This was more of a gesture than a solid achievement: for years to come Caesar, his hands full in Gaul and beset by strife at home, was in no position to enforce the treaties which had been made.

Civil strife and the burden of maintaining large armies along hundreds of miles of defensive border against the barbarians, particularly the Germanic tribes, kept his successors just as fully occupied. Rome did not even bother to ask for the agreed regular tribute from Britain, perhaps fearing that a derisive refusal would, as a matter of principle, necessitate action which the over-stretched legions were in no position to take.

Another aspect of the treaties was ignored. Tribes suffering from the renewed aggressiveness of the unruly Catuvellauni appealed for the protection they had been guaranteed. There was no response until AD 40, when the son of Cunobelinus (Shakespeare's 'Cymbeline') reached Rome to complain that he had been banished by his father and to submit himself and his case to the Emperor Gaius (Caligula). The young man assured the Emperor that Britain was in such a divided condition, with factions perpetually warring one against the other, that its complete conquest would be a simple matter. The vain, extravagant Gaius hurriedly assembled an army at Boulogne, but it mutinied and he had ignominiously to abandon his advertised invasion.

Gaius was assassinated the following year, to be succeeded by Claudius. By then 51 years of age, Claudius was at first reluctant to don the purple.

Misshapen and ailing from childhood, so that he was said by Suetonius to be at his most majestic when lying down, he preferred a secluded life as a literary dilettante, writing some comedies and a manual for dice-players, and showing no great political ambitions. Once urged to power with the support of the army, however, he decided he must make his mark. Some great expansionist gesture was needed.

Refugees from Britain continued to arrive in Rome with stories of atrocities and a country plunged into anarchy. British marauders impertinently harried the coasts of Gaul. It was not enough to drive them off and reinforce the coastal defences: such work would have to be paid for, imposing an extra tax burden on the province. It was preferable to subdue the British on their own ground and let them pay for their own behaviour or misbehaviour. Was it not time for Julius Caesar's promises to be honoured?

Claudius's wife Messalina bore him a son in AD 42, and the boy was named Britannicus. In 43 Claudius ordered the invasion of Britain.

Legions under the command of Aulus Plautius landed on the Kentish coast near Richborough, and within a few months had made such progress that Claudius himself was able to pay a fortnight's visit and place himself at the head of his troops for the advance on the tribal capital of Camulodunum (Colchester).

4
Vespasian, later to become Emperor, led the Second Legion's attack on the great ramparts and stockades of Maiden Castle in Dorset, where the last organised resistance to Roman subjection of southern Britain was offered.

5
*A Roman ballista bolt
embedded in the backbone of a
Briton slain at Maiden Castle.*

The west and north took longer to subdue, and remained a source of intermittent trouble throughout the centuries. In Wales, despite the early defeat of Caratacus, there were frequent rebellions calling for successive campaigns by successive governors of the province. Indeed, the Picts and Scots who made so many raids and forays from Ireland were never brought under the imperial rule. But in the south and south-east, and reaching out into the Midlands and East Anglia, the pattern followed the usual Roman procedure. Defeated enemies were treated leniently provided they fitted without too much complaint into the new system. Military garrisons were established at strategic points, but it had never been the conquerors' policy to keep these too expensively manned for longer than was absolutely necessary. The plan was always to encourage the native population to adopt Roman ways, and train the nobles and their brighter sons to take over the job of running their own regions, thus giving them a personal stake in the welfare of those regions and of the country as a whole. It was in the local interest to be rid of occupation forces as soon as possible and so be rid of the burden of feeding soldiers and animals, and of paying taxes for the upkeep of quarters and equipment – though of course each must contribute to the maintenance of the army in the uncivilised west and north.

Administrative centres were based on the old tribal territories, with a town as the focus of each. The earliest of these were hastily constructed of wood, often the extension of an original tribal capital. As time went on, more solid and enduring masonry made its appearance along the streets.

The Romans were essentially town-dwellers. From a military point of view they had found it sound practice to establish strongholds which in troublesome times could protect essential agricultural regions and in times of peace provide a market and civil administration offices. This policy was followed in Britain, but rather more loosely than in some other countries. Many of the native aristocracy, though paying lip service to the advantages of Roman centralisation and rationalisation, preferred to spend most of their time on their large estates where they could keep a personal eye on their labourers and crops.

6
Tombstone from the legionary fortress of Glevum (Gloucester) of a first-century cavalryman, Rufus Sita, riding down a western Briton.

In the hilly areas, the land provided only the barest living, and the inhabitants were herdsmen rather than tillers of the soil. Many led a nomadic existence, immune to the more sophisticated life style of the lowland Belgae, and had neither the wish nor the qualifications for city life and work. Towards them the Romans were tolerant on the whole, but found the relationship an uneasy one. Largest of all the tribal conglomerations in Britain, the Brigantes spread their flocks and herds between the Tyne and a line running between the Mersey and the Humber, also taking in most of the Peak District. In spite of this scattered existence, with no true capital town, and their primitive economy, the Brigantes could muster a reliable fighting force, bred the finest horses for war chariots, and were themselves skilled charioteers. Their queen, Cartimandua, had soon decided to collaborate with the Romans, probably to stave off any attempt to discipline and corral her people. When the still defiant Caratacus fled to her for refuge she showed

*7
Two Celtic deities found at Corstopitum (Corbridge). On the left is a wheel-god, possibly Tanaris, in the form of a mould which would have been used for relief decoration of pottery. The smith-god on the right, complete with hammer, tongs and anvil, is an actual* appliqué *decoration from such pottery.*

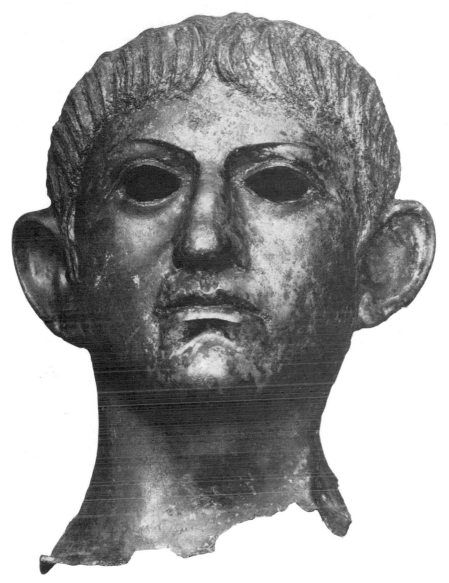

8
After his return to Rome from conquered Britain, the Emperor Claudius was accorded a 'triumph', the ritual Roman procession in honour of a victorious general. The cult of Emperor-worship was instituted at a temple in Camulodunum, from which this bronze head of Claudius was probably looted during the rebellion of the Iceni under Boudicca. It was rediscovered in this century in the river Alde, Suffolk.

her loyalty to the newcomers by handing him over. But the Romans were never quite sure where they stood with these unpredictable nomads. They allowed them plenty of leeway provided there was no real threat to law, order, and profitable trading; but were happier with those native tribes and institutions which could be incorporated tidily in their own approved framework.

In AD 78 Julius Agricola, who had earlier served in Britain as a military tribune and therefore knew the territory well, was appointed governor of the whole province. He set about acquiring some of the hitherto recalcitrant northern regions for Rome, and in order to consolidate his power over the Britons who lay to his rear he put an end to civic corruption and profiteering.

9
*Richborough in Kent:
bridgehead, supply base and
granary for the Claudian
invasion troops, reinforced in
the third century as a fort of
the 'Saxon Shore'.*

Also he was assiduous in encouraging the education and willing cooperation of the more promising natives. He, more than anyone, made it clear
that advancement under Roman rule meant town life and town ways.
Nobody was actually penalised for staying in the countryside; but nobody
could hope for increased learning, increased prosperity, or promotion
within the Romano–British hierarchy, if he did choose to shun the towns.
Agricola gave official and personal approval to the building of temples,
public meeting places, and spacious private mansions. Tacitus, his fulsome
son-in-law, wrote of him that he praised the keen and scolded the slack, and
competition to gain his approval was as effective as compulsion.

Once corrupted by the desire to emulate the Romans in speech, dress and
the acquisition of wealth, the Britons were of course caught in what we
nowadays call the rat race. The more they gained, the more they coveted.
Queen Boudicca, or Boadicea, had from the start been contemptuous of the
Romans and their British imitators as insolent and impious men – 'if these
can indeed be called men who bathe in warm water, eat delicacies, drink
wine, anoint themselves, sleep on soft couches and indulge in unnatural
vices'. Her husband Prasutagus had kept the tribal territory of the Iceni
virtually intact by becoming a 'client king' of Rome. On his death he
bequeathed the kingdom to his two daughters and the Emperor Nero, no
doubt hoping that Nero would graciously accept his share but leave the
running of it to the resident princesses. Instead, the Romans made a ruthless
takeover, raped the two daughters, and flogged the widowed Boudicca
when she tried to protest. This led to the famous bloody rebellion of the
Iceni, and its equally bloody suppression: an object lesson, from the Roman
point of view, to all other dissidents who might question imperial authority.

Most tribal aristocrats preferred to toe the line, especially after Agricola had coaxed them with promises of favours to be won. The richest joined the ranks of the decurions – 100 local dignitaries in each key town, responsible for local government within the confines of over-all imperial decrees. The bait of full Roman citizenship was dangled before those willing to devote their time and money to serving as magistrates: one needed not only a property qualification but a healthy income to meet the expenses of these honorary posts.

As the years went on, such men learned how to adjust the system to suit their wishes. Some chieftains who agreed to take over reins of office managed to do so on a part-time basis, grudgingly spending certain limited periods in town and then escaping to their estates along the vastly improved roads which were just one feature of the new régime now gradually ceasing to be new.

We have noted that, as with so many other Roman innovations, the primary function of these roads was a military one. Advancing through a new province, or hurrying to defend an old one from attack, the legions needed a dependable thoroughfare and good supply routes to back them up.

10
A bronze corn measure from the first century. The Romans turned over large tracts of land to the cultivation of grain to supply the legions in their protracted northern campaigns, and farmers had to pay a regular corn levy, the annona, *to the military authorities.*

When a region was pacified and civil authorities took over, the networks of roads remained to facilitate swift reaction to any local or widespread revolt; but were increasingly used by produce waggons and traders who found their commercial travelling much eased by such communications. There had been tribal tracks in pre-Roman times, but even when they followed much the same direction as that at which the conquerors were now aiming, the Roman engineers rarely built upon these ancient pathways. They preferred to make their own alignments by highly advanced surveying instruments used in conjunction with a sequence of beacons and smoke signals from successive high points. These trunk roads were designed to run as straight as possible: where a diversion was necessary, it tended to be made up of straight segments rather than a curve, and major changes of direction were usually achieved on hilltops.

Basic construction of these roads, whether the narrow type which could just accommodate a column of infantry, or wider ones up to 15 or 20 feet and, exceptionally, as much as 30 feet for general traffic, consisted of an *agger* or embankment, formed by digging out broad ditches on both sides of the road. The embankment itself was set on a solid foundation of large stones, usually with crushed stone rammed into the gaps, topped by layers of gravel and other chippings, depending on the most suitable local sources of supply. Roads in and about the great Kent and Sussex forest known later as the Weald were often metalled with slag from the iron furnaces. Water drained from the cambered surface of the causeway into the parallel ditches.

An impressive major road whose path can still be traced is Stane Street, which ran from Noviomagus Regnensium (Chichester) to London. Relics found on or beside this route confirm the existence of wooden bridges,

11
An aerial view of Stane Street, the Roman road from Noviomagus Regnensium (Chichester) to London.

watering troughs, posting stations, small communities serving and served by the busy traffic, and a number of villas, the largest and most celebrated being that of Bignor. Probably, too, on this as on most other main roads, there would be official collection points for the corn levy exacted by the regional government.

As tribal capital of the Regni, Chichester was already a sizeable settlement before the Romans came. King Cogidubnus had established a close liaison with them even before the invasion, and welcomed the legions on British soil. In recognition of his services he was given the title 'King and Imperial Legate' and set about building himself a superb palace whose remains can be seen today at Fishbourne.

It is significant that this rich establishment was, like most of the rural villas, the home not of an immigrant Roman functionary but of a pro-Roman Briton. Once the invaders had been helped on their way westward, leaving behind the facilities of their harbour and store base, the native ruler set himself to embellishing his city with new bridges, roads, and above all the prestige symbol of his own living quarters. Timber was replaced by masonry; plaster walls were lavishly painted; and fine colonnades were set up around the courtyard, later expanding into an ornamental garden.

12
Two Roman roads: (a) on Blackstone Edge, above Littleborough in Yorkshire, with a central trough; (b) the London to Lewes road near Holtye, East Grinstead, metalled with slag from Sussex ironworks.

Few were so wealthy as to be able to emulate a client-king of this stature, but an enterprising man could build up profitable estates and enrich his household by trade in timber, food and hides from those estates. On a smaller scale there were communities of homesteads outside the main military centres, provided for army veterans who wished, after demobilisation, to remain in the province and work allotments or smallholdings. Few aspired to the status of a villa, and indeed it is not too far-fetched to see the erections on such patches of land as allotment huts: most retired legionaries lived within the suburbs of an old garrison town and went out daily to tend such ground as had been allocated to them according to rank.

One of the first cities developed for these retired soldiers was Cunobelinus' old capital of Camulodunum. When Claudius entered the city it was no more than a sprawl of primitive hovels. Although the warrior chieftain and his leading courtiers had become wealthy enough to trade advantageously with the Romans, import a wide range of luxury goods from the rest of Europe, and strike their own valid currency, they had not yet acquired any wish to emulate Roman architecture or town planning. The conquerors at once set about transforming this Celtic capital into a recognisably Roman city with a grid-iron pattern of streets, aqueducts and municipal drainage, and solid stone houses in place of the huts and timber dwellings with which the Belgic warlords had been content. When large detachments of the army moved west to intensify the campaign against the Welsh, they left behind a nucleus of their demobilised comrades to farm allotments and maintain a patriotic presence in the region.

Provision of land for such veterans in what was called a *colonia* involved the eviction of the natives whose land this had so recently been. Dispossessed of their soil and their simple huts, these peasants now had to serve their superannuated conquerors on building sites and in the fields which had once been their own. In addition, the nobility of the tribe had to provide a devout priest and priestess for the new cult of Emperor-worship established in honour of Claudius in Camulodunum.

Similar *coloniae* were set up towards the end of the first century at Lindum (Lincoln), base of the Ninth Legion, and Glevum (Gloucester), where the troops from Camulodunum had been stationed during the major campaigns against the Silures of southern Wales.

13
The rectangular pattern of Celtic fields on Smacam Down, Dorset, often referred to as lynchets from the term for their dividing ridges, usually made by banking up stones and soil when clearing the ground, or sometimes by erecting drystone walls.

14
Aerial photography reveals the outlines of a villa in Ditchley Park, Oxfordshire. One can still clearly see the house itself and the lane leading into an enclosed yard. It has been deduced from the dimensions of its fourth-century granary that the whole estate must have covered about a thousand acres.

Older British villages and scattered farmsteads safely distant from the greedy towns were not altogether abolished or engulfed in larger units. There are indications that the Romans allowed some minor *oppida*, the old Celtic forts and earthworks, to be occupied by uncombative subsistence farmers, and in the lowlands there remained many old-fashioned settlements of wooden-floored huts on clay foundations, with walls of clay lump or perhaps wattle and daub, and roofs the same or turfed. They formed what might be classified as communal farms rather than the many-faceted villages which developed in England from medieval times onwards. Each community might aim at self-sufficiency; but many were probably incorporated in larger estates, either as tenants paying their way or as serfs.

15
Tenants paying rent.

Paying one's way was an essential in the Roman system. The individual had to justify his existence; the province had to prove its worth as a cog in the machine. Britain had been annexed partly as a result of Claudius's wish to add a name to the roll-call of Roman possessions, but also to pay for the upkeep of vulnerable frontiers and contribute to the well-being of the whole Empire. Agriculture and industry were harnessed to the imperial baggage train. First and foremost came the supply of corn, its levy written into all treaties. Agricultural production channelled through town markets and town tax offices took the place of the old hit-and-miss, largely subsistence farming of individual Celtic communities.

Larger, competently managed estates were more profitable, and the duties on their output easier to assess. Educated men made better managers and better owners. And, being educated up to Roman standards, they had higher ideals in the operation of their farms and ranches and the construction of their homes.

So began the era of villa building in Britain.

*   *   *

A few of these desirable country residences were occupied by Roman procurators and other officials, sometimes pensioned off, or by veteran army officers. Lower ranks in the army could not take their womenfolk about with them but were allowed to marry native women: if posted to another province, they tended to leave the wife and any resultant children behind and seek another consort in the next theatre of operations. Officers, however, were permitted to bring their wives to the province in which they had been ordered to serve, and after years of duty were in many cases happy to make the environment their own. Yet most functionaries probably tended to look back across the Channel when the time for discharge approached: just as the officers and civil servants of the British Raj, after years of service in an India which they understood far better than they understood England, still spoke of Surrey, Hampshire or Herefordshire as 'home'. Those Romans who chose to remain in Britain were more likely to settle in one of the *coloniae*, among folk whose language and service slang they knew off by heart, than on a working farmstead. Contrary to a belief held for some time after re-discovery of substantial villa sites in this country, the majority of these estates in the Britannic province were the property not of colonial exiles but of Romano–Britons.

To us the word 'villa' connotes a stereotyped detached or semi-detached residence in a middle-class suburb or, if we look farther afield, some snug little private retreat on a hillwide with, conventionally, a coolly shaded garden: in no sense a place of work, unless it be the home of a best-selling novelist or playwright shunning the crowds and the television studios. We would not automatically connect it with a farm and its farmhouse. But the

Latin meaning of the word is simply a farm, distinguishing it from hut settlements or town houses: not a native farm complex such as the long-established compound at Little Woodbury in Wiltshire, or the hillside terraces worked by occupants of scattered hamlets or the corners of an otherwise abandoned hill-fort, but an intensively worked farm integrated into the social and economic organisation of the Roman world. Market towns, garrison towns, military roads and rural villas belonged to the same network. In the highland zone the farmhouses tended to be made of dry-stone walls with few niceties of style or decoration, and had altered little since the decades before the invasion. In the lowlands, the influences of Rome itself and its Continental provinces showed more clearly.

Sometimes pre-Roman sites would be taken over and refashioned, or smaller and ill-coordinated agricultural settlements would be incorporated into one estate with a new central building as the administrative focus. Anyone with enough money could buy himself a villa, and some invested in more than one; but the higher authorities made it plain that they favoured serious application to the actual working of the farm. A man might be an absentee landlord, and was assuredly not frowned on for refusing to quit the city altogether – but if he was to acquire land he ought at least to learn how best to utilise that land. As *dominus*, or owner, he must not leave everything to even the most skilled *vilicus*.

Living quarters, however, did not have to be too puritanically functional. From what might at first have been no more than a purely workaday farm-house there developed the varying styles of the more luxurious villa.

CHAPTER II

THE GROWTH OF A HOMESTEAD

When a third-century man of substance purchased a villa, it might well have gone through several transmutations before coming into his hands. One may question the likelihood of different styles of house being developed upon the same plot rather than a completely fresh site being chosen for each new development, but there is evidence that this happened many times. Romans and Romano–Britons let hill-top settlements decay; but a good patch of lowland pasture has been a good investment from Celtic times onwards, and probably from even further back. A potential landowner could more readily be drawn towards estates already marked out and cultivated than towards virgin, unpredictable soil. Since the majority of Romano–British farmers were themselves of Celtic descent, they would know what their ancestors had known and be happy to adapt new techniques to old terrain.

The British farmer had for generations been content with a round hut as his home. A large farmhouse would commonly consist of a wide, circular timber wall, with timbered beams supporting a low-pitched roof of thatch or compacted turves. There was usually a hole in the centre of the roof to allow smoke from the central hearth to escape. Humbler dwellings were also circular, occasionally with drystone walls or wattle and daub. None of this was to the taste of the Romano–British magnates in search of a permanent residence in the country. One of the surest signs of their takeover is in the replacement of round huts by rectangular buildings. The fabric incorporated readily available local materials, but in general there were stone foundations, half-timbered walls filled in with wattle and daub, and a roof which may in early instances have carried thatch but was usually made of more enduring slate or tile. Native villages continued to use round huts for varying periods in different parts of the country; but even the simplest houses occupied by veterans from a *colonia* such as Lincoln or Colchester were rectangular and solidly constructed.

The earliest Roman-influenced cottages consisted of a single storey of two or three small rooms with connecting inner doorways, perhaps largely wooden at first but then strengthened by flint and mortar or some other accessible stone. Obviously there was little privacy: the rooms simply

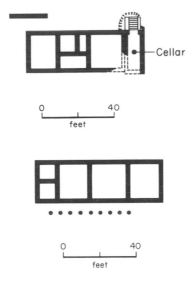

16
*Plan of the simple early cottage
at Park Street, near
Verulamium (St Albans).*

*17
Lockleys, near Welwyn in
Hertfordshire, a site known to
have been occupied from Belgic
times and on through the
Romano-British period. From
this simple layout, probably
with doorways opening from
each room into the next, evolved
a more advanced Roman house
which was destroyed by fire and
ultimately rebuilt in the fourth
century.*

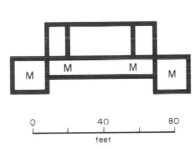

*18
A winged corridor house at
Great Staughton, west of St
Neots in Huntingdonshire. The
'M' indicates mosaic pavements,
in this case with geometric
patterns.*

opened in and out of each other. Late in the first century AD and the early second century, internal corridors with rooms to either side made their appearance; or, in many examples, there was an external veranda serving the same purpose. These so-called 'corridor houses' were in essence family dwellings on land which could be worked by one man and his wife and children, with perhaps a few labourers or slaves, accommodated in a separate shed which they might have to share with the livestock. In some regions these compact dwellings would have housed the tenants of a larger villa proprietor or an official such as the imperial procurator; in others, self-supporting peasant families.

On a more extensive estate the separate shed might become a barn of such dimensions as to be almost a house in its own right, and some farmers – or resident bailiffs – chose to lodge not only their animals and workers in such a building but also themselves and their families. These aisled houses could develop into what are known as 'basilican villas'. The roof of the large main hall was supported by two rows of pillars, giving a church-like effect of nave and two aisles. There would be at least one side entrance, and a larger opening at one end to admit waggons. Part of one aisle would be partitioned off for the family's use, while other sections were given over to the farm workers, stabling, storage of produce, and seasonal shelter for pigs and cattle. Some had kilns for drying grain.

When a new owner took over, perhaps a man like our urban official who intended to remain an absentee landlord for a considerable time, he might decide to hand over the aisled barn entirely to his bailiff and staff, and build himself a new, purely residential house on the far side of the farmyard, or maybe further away on a more attractive slope above the meadows, facing south to catch the sun and sheltering from the wind in a snug shoulder of the hill. This did not necessarily mean that he regarded his *vilicus* and other workers as being so socially inferior that they must be segregated: many landlords provided the basilican barns with comforts up to the standard of their own, including bath-houses and hypocausts for central heating – and, with an eye to practical matters, for corn-drying.

An alternative to building a new house was, as we have mentioned, to adapt one already in existence. What might originally have been only a three-roomed adjunct to the larger basilican villa now developed into the major building on the farm. The few linked rooms and their simple passage or veranda expanded to a length of a hundred feet or so, and then sprouted wings at both ends to become a 'winged corridor' villa. These end sections contained larger rooms than the original structure, and it was common for senior members of the family to occupy one end and turn the other over to younger members or, if there was no adequate barn accommodation, to the bailiff and his family. Other owners preferred different layouts, and some excavated villas show an opening up of the central section with larger dining and reception rooms, and staff accommodation in the wings. There is little reliable evidence in this country of any extensive two-storey buildings, but in view of the number which existed elsewhere in Europe, as illustrated on various murals, we may suppose that some ambitious owners built upwards as well as outwards.

19
A more ambitious winged corridor house at Mansfield Woodhouse in Nottinghamshire. The 'H' indicates a hypocaust in one wing, connected also to an added outbuilding, 'reminiscent', as Sir Ian Richmond put it, 'of the billiard-room so often added to the small country house of a well-to-do owner in the nineteenth century'. There was a mosaic floor in the dining-room, and a plain tessellated pavement along the veranda.

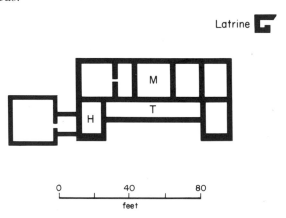

Latrine

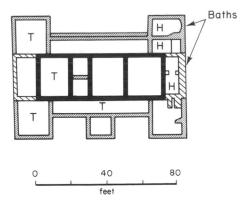

Baths

20
The winged corridor house at Hambleden, Buckinghamshire, showing later extensions to an originally simple plan.

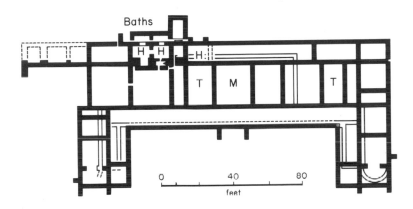

21
Development of a winged corridor house at Folkestone, Kent, into a courtyard villa.

With increasing prosperity and increasing desire to create an impression on family and friends, the owner might add yet more rooms in another wing or two at the rear of the main block. If he sold up, either because he had overreached himself or had his eye on an even more splendid property elsewhere, or perhaps because he had been promoted and posted to another city, his successor might add further limbs and reshape certain sections to suit his own tastes. Some worked on plans acquired from sketches and descriptions brought in from the Continent.

Wings could be extended until they embraced a three-sided yard before the house. Then it was logical enough to close off the fourth side with another suite of rooms. Whether this area was used for leisure purposes or as a sheltered yard for the needs of the farm depended on the owner's personal involvement in the actual management of his estate. Ambitious planning frequently produced a second courtyard enclosed by an additional range of buildings, and then there was more likelihood of one being private, the other functional. Each would be supplied with a main gate, one for animals and vehicles, the other for the family and visitors, with a porter's lodge. The stretches of living and reception rooms were bordered by cloistered or open corridors, in some sections slightly raised and reached

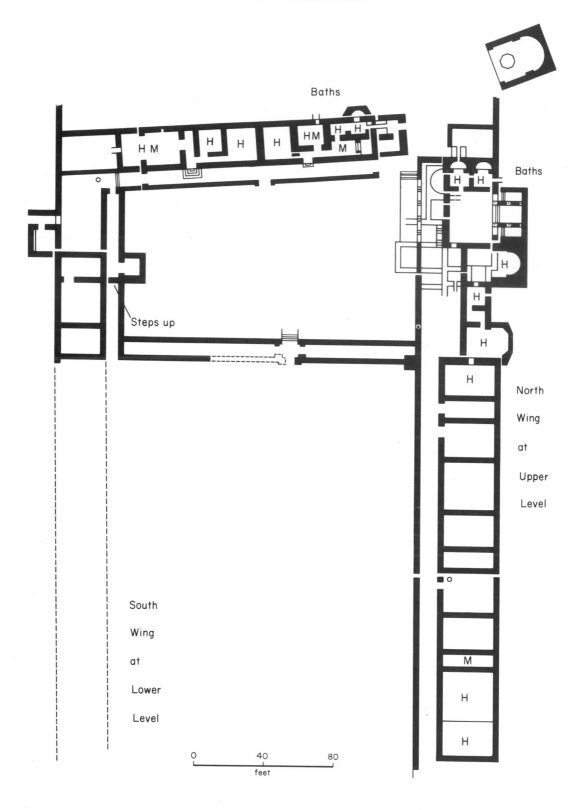

Baths

Baths

HM   H   H   H   HM   H H
                          M

Steps up

H

H

H

H

North

Wing

at

Upper

Level

South

Wing

at

Lower

Level

H

M

H

H

0   40   80
        feet

by small flights of tiled steps. If the water supply was abundant, a fountain supplied through ceramic mains might play in the centre of a formal garden.

The presence of such fountains indicates the siting of the villa near a steady water supply. Many villas relied on wells, but ideally there ought to be a flowing stream. Ducts from this would feed water to the house, its fields, and its animals. If the watercourse were wide and deep enough it might link with some of the transport canals which the Romans utilised in such areas as the Fens, or with a river also forming part of a delivery network. It seems very likely, for instance, that one section of the Lullingstone villa in Kent served as a sort of boat-house into which the river flooded at certain times, enabling grain to be loaded into boats and despatched down the Darent to its confluence with the Thames. When domestic and agricultural supplies depended on lesser brooks or springs, it was considered advisable to safeguard the source and its continuing output by erecting a small statue or shrine dedicated to the resident, beneficent nymph.

Distribution of such water supplies could often be a complicated business. There are records of waterwheels turned by slaves on a treadmill, of bucket hoists, and of the *cochlea* or Archimedean spiral screw which, despite its leaking wastage, is still used by desert tribesmen in many parts of the world: working models of the *cochlea* and a bucket hoist exist for the delectation of the young (and their guardians) in the Science Museum, South Kensington. Pliny refers to an *organa pneumatica*, which Kenneth White in his fascinating 'Farm Equipment of the Roman World' identifies with a piston pump mentioned by several other chroniclers: an example has been discovered at the bottom of a well near Silchester, that wonderfully preserved 'sylvan city' where so much was learned about Roman Britain before the contract with the landholders necessitated its re-interment below cultivable soil.

Within the house, water was needed not only for the kitchen but for facilities unknown to the Britons before the Romans came, and forgotten again for many centuries after the Anglo-Saxon invasions. Every villa of any consequence had to acquire at a certain stage of its growth a bath-house or several such houses. One feels that to any self-respecting, self-advancing Romano–Briton the well-appointed bathroom, or sequence of bathrooms, was *de rigueur* in the way that a two-car garage or, even more appropriately, a garden swimming-pool is to our contemporary suburbanite in the upper income bracket.

A simple bath-house or more lavish suite might be incorporated in one of the end wings of the main building, or set in a block of its own as a fire precaution: for these were not merely rooms for a cold tub or a cold sluicing down, but a set of hot and cold ablutions which can be described without undue facetiousness as possessing 'all mod cons'.

The simplest version might have no more than two rooms, as in the example discovered at Stonham Aspall in Suffolk. Others were more complex. A particularly luxurious villa could have a sort of Turkish bath with

22
The luxurious villa of Chedworth, Gloucestershire, beautifully situated and obviously the home of a man of consequence. The walk around the enclosed yard, partly an open veranda, suggests that this was once a garden and that if there were a working farmyard it would have been at the eastern end, between the north and south wings of outbuildings.

all its accoutrements at one end of the main block, and Swedish baths at the other or in a separate building. The commonest design began with a disrobing room from which the bather went into a cold plunge and then on through the *tepidarium*, or warm room, as a preliminary to the hot bath and steam bath. The vapour came from vessels of water above a hot flue, while the actual baths might also be positioned above a flue or even sunk into the floor itself.

Hot water and steam were usually produced by the system known as a hypocaust, installed not merely to serve the bathrooms but to warm the rest of the house – a forerunner of our modern central heating. A furnace beside the house, stoked from outside, fed heat under the raised floors and through ducts in the walls. Its fuel was usually wood or charcoal, though remains of coal stores have been identified in one or two locations. Controls were not as smoothly adjustable as our own, and changes of temperature were governed in what must have been a somewhat rough and ready fashion by calculating the amount of fuel tipped into the furnace, the strength of the draught and the weather conditions outside, and by opening or closing doors and windows.

Where the main hypocaust or a separate one could also be applied to the labourers' quarters and storerooms, as when incorporated in a basilican barn, underground flues were installed to heat kilns for the drying and parching of corn, so that the stored grain would not germinate.

23 (opposite)
Remains of the hypocaust at Chedworth, showing part of the tessellated flooring above the warm air ducts and a more recent form of heating in the top left-hand corner!

24
The structure of a hypocaust. On a cemented stone foundation (A) were laid large tiles (B), and above them a number of supporting piers (C). Square tiles (D) capped these low pillars, and some were carried across adjoining piers (E). Over this was laid the main floor, ornamented perhaps with a mosaic.

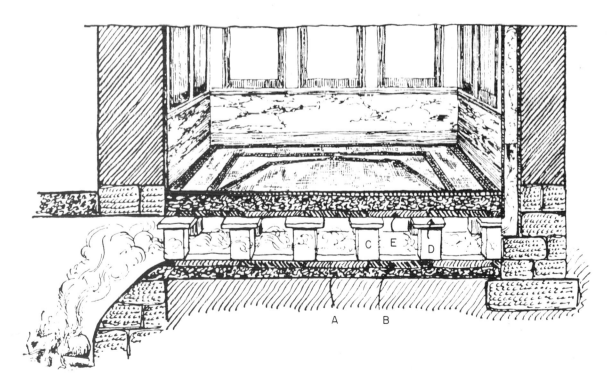

In many ways the well-to-do farmer could lead a more truly 'civilised' life than his equals in the more congested cities. Bath-houses in town were communal and not for those who valued their modesty – though mixed bathing was officially frowned on. Surviving comments on the subject leave an impression of backslapping and horseplay, bawdy shouting, and the equivalent of Rugger songs echoing out into the adjoining streets. Few towns had piped water, so for private use servants had to fetch buckets from wells and public fountains – hardly a practicable method of supplying a domestic bath-house. The farmer, in contrast, had his own uncontaminated spring, and his well-appointed bath suite. Immigrants of Roman birth and upbringing might prefer the city bustle in spite of its drawbacks. The educated Romano–Briton was more likely to remain a countryman at heart, softening such rural disadvantages as there might be by transferring a selection of modern innovations to his distant retreat.

*   *   *

In the barn, or in remote rooms in a complex villa, there would be slave quarters, distinct from the accommodation provided for hired labourers and artisans. Much of the worst drudgery, both in towns and on the estates, was performed by slaves. Even before the Romans put in an appearance the

25
An iron padlock and chain.

Belgic chieftains had made great use of forced labour on their land, and exported any surplus: indeed, many a brief border raid or inter-tribal skirmish may have been callously initiated simply in order to acquire some profitable captives, just as a hunting expedition might be mounted to acquire hides for the export trade.

It is a sad commentary on the combination of human 'progress' with human callousness that, as the Iron Age offered so many new opportunities and new techniques, an early application of those techniques was to be seen in the manufacture of chains for slave gangs. Iron padlocks of various advanced designs were made by skilled craftsmen – in some cases, doubtless, to secure doors, but in many others identifiably to secure chains and handcuffs.

One such chain, with a manacle still attached, was found during excavations at the pre-Roman farmstead of Park Street, on Watling Street near Verulamium (St Albans). Buildings here had been in use throughout Belgic times, and some finds suggest that there was a settlement on the site since the Bronze Age. The site is in fact a good example of Romano–British farmers choosing to establish themselves on and around the foundations of an existing farmhouse. Earlier huts gave way to a rectangular house with five simple rooms and a cellar. Wall plaster was colourfully decorated, and it seems fairly certain that there was a tiled roof. Altogether the new edifice was about four times larger, and undoubtedly that much more impressive in workmanship, than its predecessor.

But the slaves remained constant; or, rather, there were new generations and perhaps different races of slaves. The civilising influences which led the Romano–British to ape their conquerors and practise some of the refinements of living, including the art of philosophical conversation over the dinner table, did not extend to the treatment of those unfortunates whose labours made possible the accumulation of so much wealth. There were slaves in Rome and in the provinces, and always had been. They served as labourers and domestic staff in town and country houses, and in certain industries. The city administrator or rural landowner felt few qualms about them. You bought them at a fair price in the market-place, you treated them as you would treat your other animals – food and living conditions must be such as to keep them in good working trim – and you kept their numbers, like those of your other herds, at an optimum level.

Those who worked on a farm might not live too harsh a life, and probably fed better than many an upland peasant, or even some of their fellows in the towns; but they had no freedom of movement or employment, and were bound to their masters until such time as, maybe, the master decided to sell them off. Numbers of their children were certainly sold, after enough had been selected for farm labour. Continental market-places saw great numbers of slave children from Britain up for auction, and even after the Saxon invasions the tradition was kept up: Bede mentions English boys being sold in the Rome market in the sixth century.

26
Bronze figurines of captives, obviously destined for a life of slavery.

Surplus children, especially girls, were killed off as one might kill off a litter of unwanted kittens. Among the infant burials which examination of country villas has revealed is one of nearly 100 new-born babies beside the house at Hambleden in Buckinghamshire.

The pacification of large areas of Britain and the suppression of inter-tribal conflict meant an inevitable decline in the supply of slaves captured in local battle. Still there were many shipped south across the border with Scotland, even when the Caledonians were supposedly at war with their neighbours south of Hadrian's Wall. Trade, like rebellions and raids, went on in fits and starts: even in the most troublesome times there were enterprising traders bringing in wool, hides, and slaves. When the demand was still not satisfied, adventurous raiders made expeditions to the Irish coast. Exports of slaves from Britain to other provinces continued, as we have seen, even through the later years when Roman power was crumbling and many workers on the land were deserting their masters and going off to join robber bands. Greed for immediate cash remained, with some merchants, greater than their sense of responsibility towards the working of the land.

In due course, when the Roman grip was irrevocably weakened and the tables were being turned, raids began from the opposite direction: at the beginning of the fifth century, the son of a Roman official was snatched from his father's villa on the banks of the Severn and sold into slavery by Irish pirates – to return six years later, after escaping, and eventually to be canonised as St Patrick. By then the villas were isolated, vulnerable outposts rather than the sumptuous country homes of a complacent gentry.

27
A lamp or possibly an oil flask in the form of a sleeping child slave, found at Isurium Brigantum (Aldborough, Yorkshire).

CHAPTER III

LIVING CONDITIONS

Having arranged leave of absence for a week or two in order to visit his villa, our city dignitary and his wife do some last-minute shopping for supplies from the civic market and shops. Although their farm will provide staple foods, there are many imported delicacies, including olive oil and wine, which can be found only in a town centre; and the bailiff has respectfully sent requests for some minor items of farm equipment and one or two things for the villa kitchen.

Many of the town traders are essentially craftsmen working at the back of their premises, living and sleeping 'over the shop', and using an open counter on street level for sales and for taking orders. There are crockery, cutlery and glass on display, imported or made on the premises, and agricultural and household implements. The average shop, whether that of a specialist or merely a retailer, consists of an opening in the wall of a building block, fronted by a stone counter with a gap at one end so that the shopkeeper may move in and out of the street when necessary. It looks more like a solider version of a market stall than the sort of enclosed emporium familiar to later centuries; and there are indeed regular markets also, probably arousing the same resentment from established shopkeepers as temporary cut-price markets will always do.

Shoemakers, bakers, butchers, engravers, toolmakers and vintners all trade from very much the same sort of open frontage; some with shelves and counters piled with Samian ware or cheaper substitutes, some cobbling or hammering beyond an open doorway through which they can keep an eye on the public and on potential customers. Niches in the wall hold goods and perhaps, in an inner room, a safe for the day's takings. Apothecaries supply marked cakes of ointment for medicinal use, the inscriptions being factual – or at least direct and unadorned – rather than floridly panegyrising the product. The manufacturer and seller claims simply that this perfumed ointment is designed for scars, scratches and dry skin, and that this honey ointment will clear the eyes. Some of these patent medicines may be little better than quacks' cures, but there is a brisk trade in them, and in cosmetics, bath oils for men and women, and a number of unguents for a lady's toilet.

Having checked the loading of their purchases, our man and wife set out

in their fast two-wheeled cart, leaving the others to follow with provisions and luggage in a heavier four-wheeler.

The escaping city-dweller looks forward eagerly to the first glimpse of his property: perhaps from the brow of the low hill down which the straight cobbled road strikes at an angle. There below he can just distinguish the glint of the stream, healthily full after the spring rains, and the white walls and the red tiles of the villa roof. The pace of the horse quickens towards the end of the lane – once a mere track across the fields, before ever there was a building on the site, but now straightened out and metalled to provide easy access to and from the main road for produce waggons.

Approaching the farm buildings, the track forks. One spur turns through a gateway into the farmyard, surrounded by sheds, stables, the dairy, a threshing floor, and an aisled barn for the bailiff and his labourers. The other path leads through a more elaborate gate into an enclosed courtyard. This has become a garden rather than a yard, with a couple of bronze statues overlooking a pool and fountain in the middle of lawns and flowerbeds. Box hedges mark paths which converge on a tiled walk around the pool, and beyond them in one corner is an ornamental cluster of apple and cherry trees. The far wall of the enclosure is masked by climbing roses. In the flowerbeds, the favourites are roses, rosemary, lily, acanthus, violets and pansies.

28
The original bedding trenches of the garden at Fishbourne, Sussex, with water mains for supplying the fountains and marble basins.

An arcaded veranda runs all round the garden court, with flights of three
tiled steps leading up on each of the four sides to mosaic pavements with
geometrical designs in three colours.

It has been a dusty journey, and before the evening meal nothing could
be more welcome than a long spell in the bath-house on the corner of the

main building. After the family's last visit the furnace was cleared of wood ash and thoroughly cleaned by a slave lad sent in through the narrow stoke-hole. Earlier today it was re-lit in anticipation of their return, and although the evening shows signs of turning cool the interior of the house is pleas-antly, evenly warm.

30
A bather's strigil and oil-can.

Perhaps, to celebrate the coming holiday, they have invited guests for a few days from a villa near the posting station some miles up the road. The men exchange jokes and gossip, grumble about extra taxes levied to pay for the reconstruction of Pennine forts and the supply of auxiliary troops against the repeatedly troublesome Caledonians, recount details of their lives since they last met – the one having settled permanently to the task of tending his estate, the other still with his head half occupied by the fret of city matters – and speculate about the political situation in Rome, from where come rumours that yet another usurper has been assassinated.

They undress in the *apodyterium* and hang up their clothes on a row of hooks. Then comes the shock of the cold plunge in the *frigidarium*, followed by a rub with oils in the *tepidarium*. The hot room, or *caldarium*, has a vaulted roof painted with a swirl of sea creatures and reclining water nymphs, while from one decorated wall a mask of Neptune stares out, surrounded by nereids on sea horses and a line of gambolling tritons. Dolphins leap across another wall through writhing drifts of steam.

Here the friends sit on a bench and give themselves time to adjust to the heat. Some villas have two separate rooms at this stage, one with a hot bath sunk in the floor, and another to act simply as a *sudatorium* or sweating-room. When the sweat is well and truly rolling down the body, slaves begin carefully to scrape away dirt and grease with a scraper known as a *strigil*, its edge oiled in order not to scratch too abrasively. There is no record of any substance resembling soap having been used in these ablutions.

After the scraping and a sponging down, our bathers return to the *frigidarium* for a final plunge into cold water, and then are dried and rubbed with scented oils imported in large corded jars. Perhaps the ladies have

31
Family scenes, taken from stone tomb reliefs:
(a) Julia Velva and her family, York.
(b) Relief with mother and children.

preceded them, or will now take their turn in the baths. After that, there will be the inevitable feminine toilet: cosmetics spooned out of a variety of narrow glass bottles with *lingulae*; tweezers and bronze ear-scoops; an array of scrapers, cutters and polishers for manicuring the nails; and, to study the result, mirrors with a speculum surface of alloy – a large proportion of tin mixed with copper.

When they have all dressed, they go in to dine.

The dining-room has heating flues beneath the floor and in the walls behind the rust-red painted panels. Each of these panels is limned by a fine scrollwork border, with a fern pattern in each corner. Central medallions

32
A painted plaster fresco from Verulamium. On a purple background the overlapping octagons are limned in yellow. The central panels of each octagon frame yellow doves and two feline heads with reddish feathers.

contain alternating lilies and pink roses. Between the lower edges of these painted plaster designs and the floor is a dado of stippled imitation stone.

There are bronze, iron and wooden stools in the room, including some folding stools with leather seats. The ladies sit for a time on wickerwork chairs with curved backs, but when eating it is usual to adopt the Roman style of reclining on low wooden, leather-covered couches with legs about 12 inches high. As a rule these have headrests and footboards, and are drawn close to the similarly low table, on which may be spread a brightly patterned tablecloth. The diners prop themselves up on striped cushions stuffed with straw while eating their food and drinking their wine.

As darkness settles down, candles and lamps are lit. The pottery lamps, some standing on the table or on side tables, and some fastened to the wall, burn vegetable oil. A wick is inserted through a hole in the nozzle at one end; at the other is usually a handle so that the lamp may be carried about. There are also open containers in which tallow is burned, rather like a night-light candle.

33
Roman lamps, each showing handle, nozzle for the wick, and the opening for filling. There were also many types of open lamp, into which tallow was poured warm and allowed to set around a wick.

34
A carving in stone representing a wickerwork chair.

35
A Roman bronze stool.

a

36
A second-century bronze table from Flixborough, Lincolnshire, for holding a lamp.

37
Domestic scenes and equipment:
(a)   A first-century jug inscribed 'At London by the temple of Isis'.
(b)   A stone relief of cooking and bread-making.
(c)   A selection of cooking pots and a grid-iron.
(d)   A light green glass cup ornamented with a commemoration of a chariot-race winner.
(e)   Amphorae, for transporting and storing oil and wine.
(f)   A first-century bronze jug excavated from a well.
(g)   A bluish-green flagon of late first or early second century, found in a Cambridgeshire grave.

b

The room glows with the colours of floor and walls, reflected in a Gaulish glass flagon and the wine goblets, and striking glints from the company's bronze and bone rings, bangles and brooches.

c

d

e

f　g

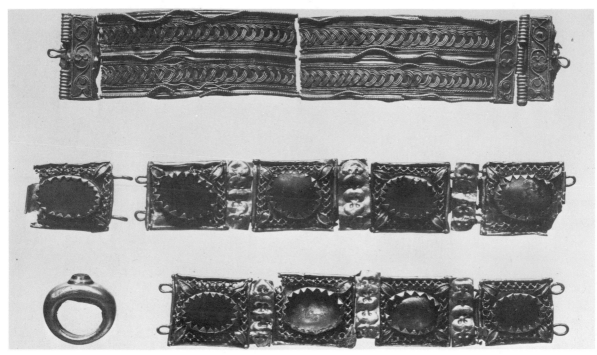

38
Bracelets, necklaces, brooches, bangles and pins.

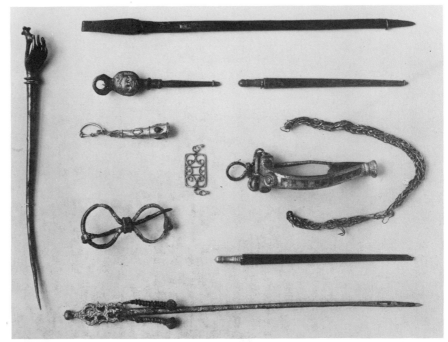

On a more formal occasion the men would wear the toga, despite some of its disadvantages in the British climate. Having described how Agricola's persuasive methods had overcome a native distaste for the Latin tongue and coaxed aspiring provincials to adopt it, Tacitus also comments: 'Our national dress came into favour, and the toga was everywhere to be seen. Thus the Britons were gradually led on to the amenities which make vice pleasurable – arcades, baths, and sumptuous banquets. They spoke of such innovations as "civilisation" when really they were only a feature of enslavement.' The toga, made from lengths of material a good three times as long as the average man, was folded over and around the shoulder and back, and bunched into folds at the front. Underneath would be a tunic – and this evening, indoors in the warmth, both men and women have contented themselves merely with tunics. A higher magistrate would be entitled to a purple hem to this garment. The women's model of sleeved tunic, known as the *stola*, was longer and had a flounce to drape about the ankles.

The lady of the house has devoted quite some time to her elaborate Roman-style coiffure with ornamental bone hairpins set around the top like a diminutive crown, and is really happier when sitting back in a chair than stooping over the bowls and platters on the low table. The wife of their guest turns from time to time towards the nearest lamp so that its light may strike sparks from the golden links of her pendant, inset with coloured beads and, at the clasp, two pearls. All of them have ornamental brooches for fastening their clothes: one a green dragonesque safety-pin brooch in the old native tradition, another an imported cloisonné *fibula* with an inset figurine.

Light gleams also in the silver tableware. Every household aspires to acquire such a set – for aesthetic reasons, prestige reasons, and for its sheer commercial value: many a splendid plate has its weight engraved on it like a hallmark.

a

39
Examples of Whitby jet:
(a) a pin; (b) a pendant.

b

At the feet of the diners begin the patterns of an intricate mosaic. A few paces in from the doorway is a depiction of Orpheus with his lute, as if serenading the company from a deferential distance. A rapt circle of birds and beasts are caught in the spell of his music. Others approach through the design as if creeping out of hiding from beneath the dining table.

Next door is the kitchen. Cooking is carried out on a raised open hearth, the charcoal being burnt in small cavities sunk into the brickwork, across which is formed a grid on which meat can be grilled or a cauldron brought to the boil. Most of the cooking vessels are earthenware, but an iron cauldron can be hung when required from hooks above the hearth or, in place of an oven, set on legs over the fire and then covered with a lid on which a smaller supplementary fire is laid. There are a kneading table, a shallow stone sink, a stone hand quern for making flour, the ubiquitous pestle and mortar for pounding seeds, spices and other ingredients, the bronze *patella* or saucepan, skillets, pewter plates, pottery mugs and pitchers, and a wide selection of knives: even the folding pocket-knife is already in common use. Supplies of olive oil and wine are stored in large jars or *amphorae*.

Food is plentiful and varied. A host of good standing can offer his guests, largely from his own resources, geese, game, chicken, kid, pork and most of our present-day meats, with a good choice of vegetables. The potato has not yet been discovered, but there are peas, carrots and cabbage; and the Romans have introduced the turnip to this country, acceptable in their own diet and invaluable as winter feed for cattle.

On a semi-formal occasion such as this one a meal may be served in three parts, beginning with eggs and shellfish. Whatever else it may lack where the discriminating palate is concerned, Britain offers the most highly prized oysters and mussels. The second course is split up into a number of different dishes, with plenty of meat: venison and roast boar may be on the menu, and although beef and mutton have never been favourably regarded in Rome itself they are a staple diet in this country. Finally there are the desserts: fruit, puddings and pastries. Most country households, naturally, bake their own bread, and our host's cook has a delightful speciality in spiced loaves and honey cakes.

The main implements used at table are the fingers. Spoons are provided, and probes for digging shellfish out of their carapaces; and we have already seen that knives are in common use. But there is no such thing as a table fork.

*   *   *

Looking benevolently down on the dining table and on other rooms and corridors in the house are a number of small bronze statuettes. These represent the *Lar*, the ancestral family spirit, and the *Penates* or household gods. Fire is eternally the symbol of Vesta, spirit of the hearth; Janus is the keeper of the door, forever looking both ways at once; and the *paterfamilias*, head of the household, is in effect resident priest to these deities, his own birthday being also celebrated as a religious festival.

To ensure the continuing protection of his gods, the Roman landowner dedicates his first crops to them and sacrifices his first-born sheep or ox of the season. Nature worship is strong throughout the land, and different communities have adopted the worship of major or minor deities who have taken their fancy: some elevated to the pantheon from their original humbler status as local patron wood or water spirits, others brought in by the Romans and especially by much-travelled legionaries. In Chichester is a temple dedicated to Minerva and Neptune; at Bath, a characteristically Romano–British compromise has been reached in the tactful compounding of a Celtic water spirit and the Roman goddess of wisdom and the arts to produce Sulis-Minerva; and Mithras and Hercules have acquired many followers.

40
A goddess and two water nymphs, from Hadrian's Wall, each symbolically pouring water from an urn and holding up a beaker.

The cult of Mithras, Persian god of light and fertility, was carried across the Roman Empire largely by legions returning from the East, he being also guardian deity of armies. He is generally represented as a handsome young man in a Phrygian cap, killing a bull, as in the Mithraeum at Vercovicium (Housesteads) on Hadrian's Wall. There is also an extensive Mithraeum in Londinium.

Hercules has become a favourite among the farmers of southern Britain, and it is probably in his honour that the prosperous Romano–British agricultural community of the vales and slopes around what will one day be known as Cerne Abbas have carved the giant figure of a club-bearing fertility symbol out of the hillside – a giant whose worship will not cease with the departure of the Romans but continue through centuries of maypole celebrations and festivals within the sacred enclosure.

Private and public religious observances shade into one another, most of them connected with the land and the cycle of seasons. The *Ambarvalia*, or blessing of the crops, takes place in May, when a procession follows a

41
A marble head of the god
Mithras found in a temple
excavated at Walbrook,
London, during the building of
a new office block in the middle
of the twentieth century.

symbolic victim round the fields, singing the praises of Ceres and Bacchus: obviously a precursor of the Christian ceremonial of Rogation days and 'beating the bounds'. And of course, as in every religion in the world, there is a harvest festival.

The cities have temples for communal worship, including the enforced cult of Emperor-worship, but out here in the countryside there are no such things as parish priests. One does not walk up the road to church in one's Sunday best. Respects to the gods are paid in private rituals, though in devout households these may well be on a lavish scale.

Our host built, a few years ago, a temple-cum-mausoleum on a mound behind the house, in which to inter the bodies of a much loved younger brother and his wife, both stricken by fever while the young engineer was supervising drainage work in the Fens. The death came tragically soon after their wedding, which took place in the city. Those present this evening had

42 (below right)
A gilded bronze statuette of Hercules.

43 (below left)
The Cerne Abbas giant, Dorset, probably a local farming community's testimony to the power of Hercules over their lives and lands.

all been in the procession which followed the young bride from her father's home to that of the bridegroom, accompanied by young folk chanting nuptial hymns. The night before, the girl had left her toys and maiden vestments in the care of the household gods and now was to become the woman of another household. In the bridegroom's home the two had solemnly joined hands and offered prayers to the gods, and then the marriage contract was signed and witnessed.

And now they lie within the tomb.

It is against Roman law to bury the dead inside city boundaries, so cemeteries and individual burials are to be found strung out along the main roads out of the city, marked by ranks of tombstones, to remind the voyager of the inevitable end of every journey. If you are afraid that by the time of your death you will be unable to leave enough money to pay for a worthy funeral, it is possible to pay regular contributions into a burial society.

During some periods the entombment of the corpse itself was favoured; during others there was a tendency towards cremation and the keeping of ashes in funerary urns or glass jars; and sometimes both customs existed side by side.

44
A crematory 'face urn' within a tile box, from Camulodunum.

45
A stone sarcophagus, its ends carved with the representation of a lion savaging a goat.

Unlike the city dweller, the villa owner can choose to keep his departed dear ones close to him. The funeral ceremony of the brother and his wife began with the bodies laid out on biers in the house, with torches burning at each corner of each bed. Money was placed in the mouths of the dead to pay for their journey into the unknown. From the house the bodies, accompanied by mourners and musicians, went up the hillside above the villa to a pyre where they were incinerated, the ashes returning at last to the specially built temple and being set in a small shrine in finely wrought and embellished pots.

Other bereaved folk might decide not to cremate their loved ones but to inter them in similar temples. In such cases the bodies might be sealed in lead and then placed in a wooden or stone sarcophagus, accompanied by cutlery, glasses and a flagon for refreshment during the journey, and perhaps a set of glass gaming pieces to divert the traveller on his way.

46 *Terra-cotta figurines from a child's grave at Camulodunum, probably caricatures of diners and a reciter, imported soon after the foundation of the* colonia.

In the case of our sorrowing older brother, a central cult room and a wooden encircling arcade were set up on a flint and mortar foundation. Each year a private ceremony is observed, with the pouring of wine and water as a libation into one of the votive pots set in the floor. These pots were consecrated at the time of the funeral and thereafter cannot be neglected: annually there must be the re-dedication ceremony, offering sustenance to the dead and appealing for benevolence towards the living.

47
The Chi-rho *monogram, one of the earliest Christian symbols to make its appearance in the decorative arts, here seen on a pewter dish.*

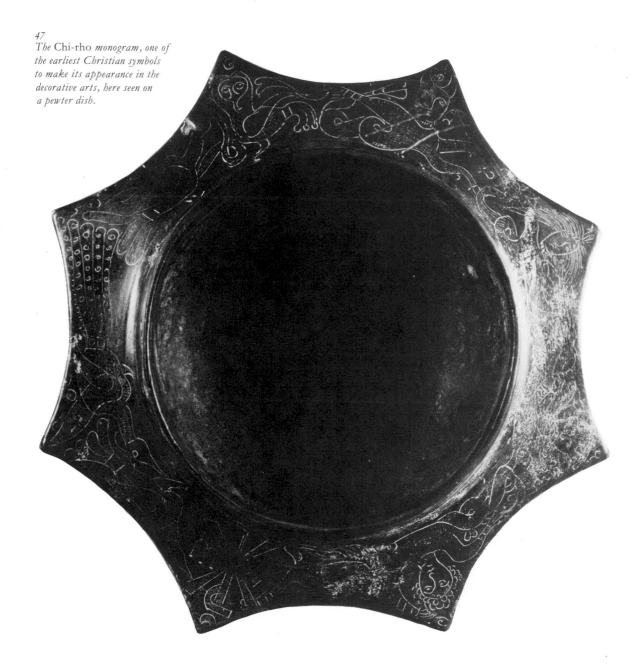

Perhaps in later years, when our landowner has bequeathed his property to his son and it has passed on to grandson and beyond – for villas can legally be bought, sold or inherited very much as in the still remote twentieth century – there may be a change in this pattern of worship: at first a curious, tentative change. Constantine the Great, who proclaimed himself Emperor at York in AD 306, was converted to Christianity while waging war against a rival contender for the imperial purple. He adopted as his emblem the *Chi-rho* monogram, the two initial letters of the Greek word for Christ forming one of the earliest of all Christian symbols. This appeared on Constantine's coinage and on the shields and standards of his legionaries. When his subjects followed his lead and accepted baptism, some of them set up chapels to the new deity and incorporated the *Chi-rho* in paintings, stonework, or mosaic inlays. At Chedworth in Gloucestershire, the stone rim of the *Nymphaeum* guarding the villa's essential spring displays the monogram carved three times into what had once been dedicated to a water nymph.

But there was no immediate scurry to dismiss the older gods too ungraciously. It was as well to hedge one's bets. Two chapels might exist side by side, one with a Christian altar and the other retaining the trappings of paganism.

One wonders whether, at the end of an evening meal and before going to bed, a household of this kind might have some equivalent of family prayers. But attempts to equate such a family with a Victorian one are at best fruitless and at worst badly misleading.

*   *   *

Meal and conversation concluded, our visitors are shown to the guest rooms. It is common for Romans and Romano Britons to sleep on the floor, sometimes on a slightly raised wooden dais with a mattress and warm blankets. Some, however, favour low-slung beds of leather thongs woven criss-cross within brightly painted wooden frames, the whole set on squat painted legs. Headboards are embellished with coloured veneers and inlays, and the blankets and coverlets present a clash of purple, brown and yellow. Some of this furniture and textiles may have been made on the premises. Every estate aims to be as nearly self-sufficient as possible, and the landowner likes to employ his own weavers, fullers, dyers, carpenters and smiths if he can afford them. Where the farm can more accurately be called a ranch, there are all the facilities for rearing sheep, shearing them, weaving what is needed for the household, and selling the surplus.

Next morning the usually absentee landlord decides to make his presence felt. He checks the accounts with his bailiff before setting off on a tour of inspection.

48
(a) Above right: a wooden
writing tablet with the branded
inscription 'Issued by the
Imperial Procurators of the
Province of Britain', and
(b) (left) various styli for
impressing characters into the
waxed surface.

Written records such as deeds of sale and inventories are made out in ink
with a reed quill or metal pen on parchment or papyrus. Some metal pens
have a small spoon-like tang at one end for stirring the ink in its pottery
inkwell. For more casual notes or correspondence, a metal stylus is used to
cut words into a wax coating on thin wooden tablets, hinged so that the
waxed surfaces can be folded inwards, fastened, and even sent through the
mail. When the message has been deciphered, the wax can be smoothed
over and used again.

Satisfied that the accounts are in order, the owner strides out across his
property accompanied by his guest, the bailiff, and his dog. Out of doors the
bailiff wears a heavy home-made hooded cloak like a duffle coat; each of the
other two has donned a *paenula*, a sleeveless square of cloth falling over the
shoulders, with a hole for the head and a hood stitched on at the back.

Crops from the fields, wool from sheep, and meat and hides from
slaughtered animals are treated and stored in the farmyard complex, where
there are a threshing floor, corn-drying kilns, and a small granary. Among
the crops introduced to Britain by the Romans have been rye and oats, but
wheat and barley are still the main produce.

A lot of the day-to-day work within these buildings, quite apart from
baking and cooking and other domestic chores, is carried on by the women
and children of the labourers and slaves. In winter, when work in the fields
is limited, the men will join them on a number of indoor tasks. There are
running repairs to be carried out on farm and domestic equipment. The
carpenter will make and mend furniture, and work on hurdles or new gates;
replacements are needed for broken pots or baskets; tools need to be cleaned
and sharpened. The women are practised in the weaving of reed and willow
into baskets and beehives, and in the fulling, dyeing and weaving of cloth.

49
At work on the estate.

As an estate prospers and the buildings multiply, a complete laundry room may be installed with a hypocaust extension or possibly a separate fire of its own, set under an inverted brick hemisphere holed like a colander, across which garments can be spread to air and which can also be used in the drying and bleaching of cloth.

On their inspection of the premises, the bailiff suggests the installation of a donkey-driven mill. The owner silently does a profit and loss calculation as he paces across the fields; and then is distracted by the sight of a gate sagging from one twisted hinge. Another urgent job for the carpenter – and, if the hinge is broken, for the smith.

Between them his carpenter and smith fashion fences, gates, furniture, spades, ploughshares and other implements. Most of our everyday tools and farm and domestic equipment were already in use by the Celts, but the Belgae and now the Romans have developed and strengthened many of them. The carpenter has his chisel, plane, saw, adze, axe and hammer. The legionaries brought with them sturdier rakes and scythes, iron-tipped

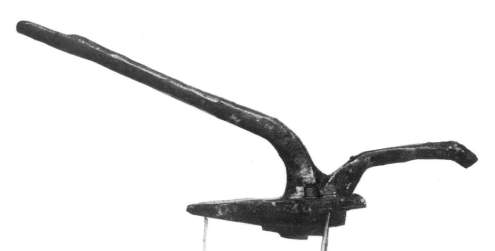

50
Bronze model of a plough.

spades and entrenching tools which the local farmers have used and adapted for their own needs.

Testimony to the existence of skilled leather workers will endure for archaeologists to rediscover in the shape of leather shoes, slippers and clothing, together with the awls and needles necessary for stitching.

51
Bronze model, about two inches high, of a ploughman and his two oxen, found at Magis (Piercebridge, Co. Durham).

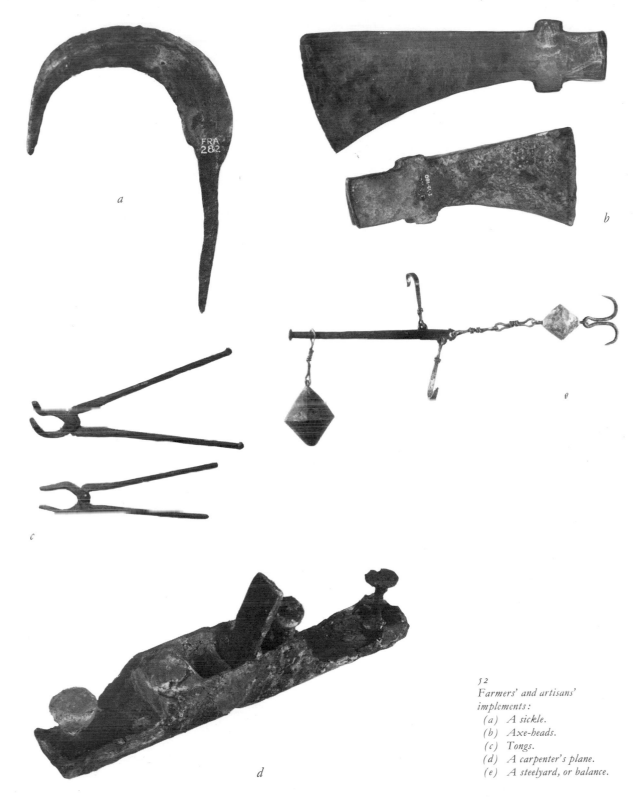

52
Farmers' and artisans'
implements:
  (a) A sickle.
  (b) Axe-heads.
  (c) Tongs.
  (d) A carpenter's plane.
  (e) A steelyard, or balance.

a

53
Viniculture
  (a) *A wine-growing estate.*
  (b) *Grape pipe thought to be
       left over from local
       wine pressing have been
       found at Calleva
       Atrebatum
       (Silchester); but these
       silver fir wine barrels
       from the same region
       were probably used for
       shipments of Bordeaux
       wine.*
  (c) *A funerary wood
       engraving of a vigneron
       and his tools.*

b

Ex eodem Cœmeterio.

Wood is plentiful, malleable iron less so. The blacksmith does not attempt anything too formidable on the farm. He may manufacture his own padlocks and keys, chains, bolts, knives, and nails of all sizes. But bringing the necessary loads of iron and the equipment for a full-scale forge to the site is too laborious and expensive, and certain heavy or complicated items are imported ready-made. Only, perhaps, in villas or villages near the forest iron workings may more ambitious constructions be undertaken.

A craftsman on the farm cannot remain exclusively devoted to his own profession. Few establishments are big enough to support full time specialists, and the artisan must be able to turn his hand to a number of other seasonal tasks when the need arises.

Sticks, poles and props of varying dimensions are cut and trimmed for the vegetable garden and the vineyard, often by lamplight so that no hour of the short winter day is lost; and where vines are to be trained up a wall or require a complicated series of experimental trellises, these can be cut and assembled according to expert advice.

We use the word 'experimental' because there still seems no guaranteed way to success with viniculture in Britain. The loving specialist finds himself thwarted time and time again. In the early days of settlement Tacitus declared that, though British soil was admirably fertile, it could not produce the olive or the vine – two essential contributions to the Roman gourmet's diet. And it begins to look as if Tacitus was right. Grapes which produce excellent wine without too much trouble in other provinces, even in some northern outposts, have proved wayward and unfruitful here. Yet one must persevere. The Romans themselves, and the Romano–British, do not

*54
Marble group of Bacchus and
companions, showing the vine
and serpent, and the remains of
a faun's leg in the tree: from
the Walbrook Mithraeum,
London, now in the Guildhall
Museum.*

regard traditional British brews as a reasonable substitute for wine. Ale
was drunk in Britain before the Romans came and continues to be so. There
is also mead, still a favourite with the natives: its essential ingredient, honey,
is produced in vessels which archaeologists of later centuries will be able to
identify confidently as beehives on several villa sites. But the landowner and
his friends demand wine; and it will help in the balance of payments if,
instead of importing it from Iberia or from the mother country itself, it can
be produced in vineyards on the slopes above one's own villa.

Greek cultivation of the vine, adopted by the Romans, moved on from them via Marseilles into Gaul. Conditions there proved so congenial that the imperial authorities, alarmed by the threat to their indigenous wine trade, enforced prohibitive treaties on tribes who wished to live at peace with them and, when war or rebellion led to the defeat of those tribes, made sure that restrictive trading clauses were written into the terms of surrender. By the first century AD, vineyards occupied so much of the time of workers throughout the Empire, out of all proportion to the cultivation of desperately needed wheat, that Domitian ordered the uprooting of all plantations outside Italy itself. This decree was never enforced as ruthlessly as he would have wished, but it seems likely that no fresh vineyards were authorised or attempted until in the third century Probus granted Gaul, Spain and Britain permission to establish their own vineyards.

In Britain there are many frustrations; but we may assume that any landowner worth his salt – if that is the right word in such a context – will set to and, as part of his private gardening programme, endeavour to coax such wine grapes as he can from this unaccustomed soil.

Strabo referred to 'clever hunting dogs' as one of Britain's main exports before the Romans took over, and it may be that our landowner will take his guest hunting during his stay. There is a profusion of deer and wild boar in the extensive forests, providing a welcome addition to the pleasures of the table; and for severely practical reasons as well as for the sport of it, regular expeditions against predatory wolves and foxes around the estate are essential. Yet hunting, like the cultivation of the vine, somehow never seems quite to have become such a favoured diversion with the Romano–British as with other provincial peoples.

55
An engraved glass bowl, probably imported from Cologne, showing a huntsman and hounds pursuing a hare.

56
Model of a boar.

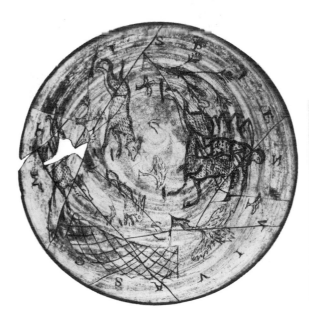

When the men return to the house and their womenfolk, or when in a male drinking session they have over-indulged in whatever liquor is available, do they ever indulge in what we might call a musical evening? Another unrewarding speculation, unfortunately: the Romans seem to have had no way of transcribing their music, and it is impossible now to hear the echoes or conjecture what sort of sound, what blend of voices and instruments, they liked best.

57
A mosaic pavement from East Coker depicting the triumphant return from the chase.

CHAPTER IV

FIXTURES & FITTINGS

Today we are in sight of AD 2000. Of these 2000 years of British history it is worth remembering that fully one-fifth were lived under the *pax Romana* and under lingering Roman influences. By the end of the first two centuries of that long domination, for most people in, at any rate, the southern low-lands there must have been a sense of security and inevitability amounting almost to smugness. Those with wealth found it comparatively easy to acquire even more wealth and to ensure themselves an ever-improving standard of living. Their outward trappings became more splendid. They not merely built and rebuilt their town houses and country homes on a grander scale but decorated them more and more lavishly.

The Romano–British who had acquired a taste for beautiful *objets d'art* and some of the more practical trappings of civilisation had at first to import them. Then craftsmen from Gaul and Italy followed the settlers and established their schools in Britain. The British themselves learned from these masters and began to work similarly in stone, iron and bronze, adapt-ing their native techniques and designs, fashioning their everyday domestic ware more gracefully, and creating their own individual frescoes. Villas in the neighbourhood of certain large towns could call on the services of what were virtually firms of painters and decorators, many with their own distinctive mannerisms and trade-mark.

It is difficult to reconstruct, either literally or in the mind's eye, a complete inner wall of a room just as it would have been in Romano–British times. When abandoned villas decayed or were burnt down and trampled over by marauders, the coloured plaster crumbled all too easily, especially if left exposed to the air. To match colours and design details from a thousand fragments of excavated wall surface, not knowing how many missing pieces may have been ground into the dust, is one of the most tormenting jobs in the world. But painstaking work and careful deduction have produced some reasonable reassemblies.

The majority of villa walls were made up of timber supporting wattle and daub. Mortar was laid over this, and a further top-coat provided the surface for painting. A foundation colour may in many instances have been applied while this surface was still wet, and the ornamentation added later. Enough examples survive for us to be able to conjecture that division of the wall patterning, vertically and horizontally, was not too remote from our own proportions. Where most modern houses have a skirting-board, the villa would sport a painted dado reaching some two to three feet up from floor level, perhaps veined in imitation marbling. The main expanse of wall was frequently divided into panels, not by raised bevelling or wooden frames, but by painted lines and scrolls, the more ambitious specimens enclosing patterns of concentric circles, whorls and loops, or flower motifs, sprays of leaves, and swags. Above, at what we would think of as picture-rail level, there might be a frieze leading on to a decorated ceiling – though remains of such ceilings have been the poorest of all survivors, and there is no hard and fast evidence on this score.

Many colours had to be imported. Others were mixed on the spot. Red derived from iron oxide, yellow from a blend of chalk and green sand, blue from copper silicate, and others from various powdered earths and vegetable dyes. Black from powdered charcoal could be blended to give different strengths and hues.

Unlike the portraits, lavish representational scenes, and *trompe-l'oeil* such as one finds in the later days of Pompeii, few identifiable figures of animals or human beings have survived in Romano–British murals, having apparently been reserved for mosaic pavements and floors, where classical themes predominate, though perhaps devised in conjunction with sylvan patterns on the plaster.

By the close of the second century it had become well-nigh obligatory for persons of consequence to vie with one another in the extent and splendour of their mosaic flooring. At the end of the third century this craft entered a new phase. Here as in other fields, British students of Continental masters refined their own techniques and styles, and a number of centres began to supply surrounding districts. Some had recognisable characteristics and specialised in certain themes – such as the familiar one of Orpheus within clusters of birds and animals, employed by what must have been a flourishing workshop at Cirencester.

Mosaic work seems to have been an invention of the ancient Greeks, who first studied its possibilities by sinking pebbles of different colours into a bed of resinous cement to form geometric or pictorial patterns. The irregularity of such natural pebbles, and the resulting unevenness of surface, led to experiments with pieces of marble, glass and ceramic, until finally it became customary to cut the pieces, or *tesserae*, to a specific standard size, usually into half-inch cubes. This knapping was carried out with the insertion of an axe-shaped chisel blade set into a wooden block, cutting edge upwards. The worker would then hold a length of stone across the sharp blade and tap off the required segments with a hammer.

Ideally the mosaic patterns should be formed by the use of naturally coloured stones – preferably, for economic reasons, from not too widely

58
'Winter' from a pavement depicting the Seasons in the Chedworth villa, Gloucestershire, the work of a school of mosaicists at Corinium (Cirencester).

59
A geometric mosaic.

scattered sources – set off perhaps by the introduction of cubes of man-made brick and tile to complement the rusty sandstone, different hues of lime-stone, and marble when it was obtainable. Some designs were austerely black and white, relying for their effect on the quality of the composition itself; but a corridor thus laid out might lead to the calculated contrast in one of the main rooms of a multi-coloured representation of gods and goddesses, animals, the seasons, Bacchus garlanded with vine leaves, or Cupid with gladiators. Family rooms would have attractive scenes commissioned on themes dear to husband and wife, or in tribute to their chosen spirit or deity; but the most sumptuous effect was generally reserved for the *triclinium*, or dining-room, where it was most likely to impress visitors. Resort to classical subjects, scenes from the poets, and figures from legend was in itself an additional boast, intimating that the villa owner who had ordered such interior decoration must be a thoroughly Romanised, well-educated and appreciative citizen of the Empire.

b

60
(a) & (b) Details from the rarely exposed pavement at Woodchester, Gloucestershire.

61 (Left)
A panel from a second century mosaic at Fishbourne showing a winged Cupid on a dolphin, the design being executed in various shades of red and yellow against a largely black and white ground, with black sea horses and red, yellow, black and white sea panthers.

New owners might have new ideas about what lay underfoot, just as a modern householder buying a bungalow will want to replace or to some extent trim or cover parts of his predecessor's fitted carpet. At Withington in Gloucestershire, for example, the border of a mosaic depicting Orpheus was apparently taken out by a later proprietor to make way for Neptune; and there are indications elsewhere of floral and geometric additions being made to mosaic panels – to extend a design, or add some personal fancy.

When Christianity spread through the land there were many such hasty readjustments, as well as a body of newly commissioned work. Pagan figures were crudely or subtly adapted to the new terms of reference. One has a vision of some hapless group of mosaicists who, having measured a job, calculated the number and colours of cubes needed, quoted a fee, and completed trimming the stones, have suddenly been told that their client has been converted to Christianity since placing his order and would now like a new approach to the picture – but without, if possible, too much wastage of prepared material and too much extra expense.

The *Chi-rho* monogram crept into pavements, and a head which might originally have been intended as Ceres or Mercury was refashioned as that of Christ. An impressive early Christian pavement with the *Chi-rho* symbol behind a face of Christ, and four figures which could be interpreted either as pagan survivors or, it has been suggested, four evangelists, is that discovered at Hinton St Mary in Dorset, now on display in the British Museum.

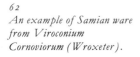

*62
An example of Samian ware
from Viroconium
Cornoviorum (Wroxeter).*

Another domestic taste was for *terra sigillata*, a pottery in which both paste and glaze were of a rich, dusky red. Known also as Samian ware, it took this name for somewhat tenuous reasons from the Aegean island of Samos, although in fact it seems to have developed from a style founded at Arretium (Arezzo) in Italy. The finest examples came originally from Italy, but the clay most suitable for its production was plentiful in Gaul, and it was from there that most British imports came, there being no equivalent clay in this island. By the first century AD the factories of La Graufenesque in southern Gaul were mass-producing Samian ware on a vast scale: it was recorded that 30-odd men in one workshop alone manufactured over 400,000 vessels between them. There were a number of standardised shapes, and the potters often stamped their names on the finished product, so that even today it is not difficult to track down the source of individual pieces.

A characteristic of Samian ware is the imitation of relief figures on silverware. The silversmith hammered out such figures. The potter, however, achieved his results by preparing decorative moulds and packing the clay into them. Many of these moulds were prepared by stamping with readymade dies carrying a range of floral emblems and occasional human and animal figures, which could be used repetitively or in different combinations as desired.

Attempts were made in the second century to establish a rival British industry at Colchester, with little success. When the Continental frontiers of Rome were pushed back by barbarian assaults in the third and fourth centuries, most of the Gaulish factories were destroyed or abandoned, and another British attempt to produce a substitute Samian ware was made around Oxford, using artificial colouring and then glazing it to match as closely as possible the real thing. There were also some short-lived factories at York and elsewhere. Some attempts were made to cut corners by stamping designs flat on to the vessel instead of moulding them. In the absence of the real status symbol, British pastiche did at last achieve some limited success.

Other indigenous products included Castor ware, grey or slightly coppery in hue, imitating the Samian appearance but with its ornamention piped on, as with a birthday or wedding cake, instead of being moulded. Many coarser pots, bowls and tankards were produced in different regions for general use. The most important and widespread, for practical rather than aesthetic reasons, was the thick kitchen *mortarium* or mortar, its inside roughened by the addition of grit to the clay before firing, to provide a grinding surface for the contents.

Romano–British glass furnaces, producing mainly window glass, have been identified in Norfolk and the Midlands, and there was one very busy factory in the garrison town of Veratinum, guarding the strategically important ford across the river Mersey at what is now Warrington. But the glass flagons and goblets used at the most discriminating tables, and the scent and salve bottles of a lady's toilet, were mainly imported from Syria and further east, until craftsmen in northern Gaul and the Rhineland applied themselves to perfecting their art and became the main suppliers. Bowls, beakers and cremation jars could have cut facets or be decorated with moulding, fluting, and ornamental medallions fixed to the blown glass. Wine glasses originally had flat bases, but then some were produced with squat feet. Stemmed glasses as we know them, however, were rare.

Craftsmen in small local workshops doubtless attempted copies of the more delicate ware brought in from other provinces, but on the whole it can be safely supposed that their main output was that of the simplest, most purely functional vessels. Some workers did not even stay in one place, but travelled in groups from one region to another, constructing a simple furnace at each stopping-place and turning out whatever was locally required until the demand was filled and it was time to move on again.

63
A Castor-ware beaker, in a style developed from Rhenish models but probably a product of the Nene valley potteries near Peterborough.

Plaster, pottery and glass are all too easily shattered in any destruction or slow collapse of a building, and only by a stroke of good fortune can substantial remains be found in good preservation or at any rate in fragments large enough to be satisfactorily restored. Copper and bronze stand up better to the ravages of time, and among the most extensive finds in archaeological digs have been personal adornments such as bracelets, clasps and brooches. Many of these *fibulae*, or brooches, based on the familiar safety-pin principle, would look perfectly at home today as, in current jargon, a fashion 'accessory'.

Later Iron Age traditions remained strong in the design of brooches, characterised by styles known from their appearance as 'trumpet' and

64
A Castor-ware kiln.

'dragonesque', often with enamelled decoration much admired by inhabitants of the other Roman provinces. Then gradually those other provincials began to take over the market with their 'crossbow' brooch. Distinctions between the various basic constructions and various makers, and sub-divisions within those basic styles, were painstakingly classified by R.G. Collingwood in his 'Archaeology of Roman Britain', and although subsequent research has suggested a few amendments, his findings are still worth the closest study by anyone interested in the progress of metal and jewellery design. From the simplest one-piece fastener to the elaborately patterned Romano–Celtic 'S-brooch' with a dragon at each end, one can follow the makers' divergent inspirations and experimentations.

There was also a fashion for brooches, ornaments and diminutive figurines in Whitby jet. This black lignite was much prized in the form of interlinked flexible necklaces, hairpins, and family portrait medallions. In this industry at least there was no question of adapting foreign models: it was an indigenous Romano–British craft, and the products of the York workshop were exported ready-made to the Rhineland, where there is no known trace of any local manufactory or school of copyists.

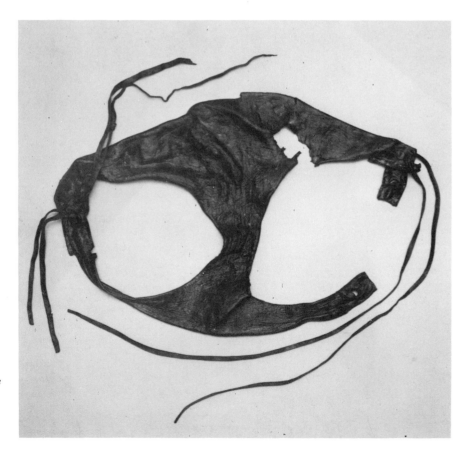

65
First-century leather trunks with a remarkable similarity to the modern bikini, found in a London well. Mosaics of similar garments are to be seen in the Piazza Armerina villa, Sicily.

Clothing must, by and large, have been locally tailored for the local climate. British cloth won and for a long period maintained a high reputation throughout the Empire: as in the Middle Ages, wool was then one of the country's most profitable commodities. Flax was grown in some districts and would have been used in the manufacture of linen. We have noted that adoption of the toga was normal in high society and among those aspiring to reach the upper financial and administrative echelons; but for the working farmer, artisan, carter or countryman in general it would hardly have been a practicable everyday garment. The weavers of the villas, and later of small industrial communities, created many warmer and more sensible things, including the highly esteemed and highly priced *birrus Britannicus*, a hooded cloak like our modern duffle coat, and the *tapete Britannicum*, a travelling rug useful for both saddles and couches.

Fulling and dyeing might be carried out efficiently on the larger estates. In the towns there were certainly full-scale establishments for the treatment of woven cloth, combining the functions of a laundry, dyer's, and dry cleaner's. At Silchester, remains of brick furnaces rather like old scullery coppers seem to have belonged to dyers' premises, where woad and madder were used for colouring. Woad, which had been much used by Britons to paint themselves a fierce near-indigo colour, continued to be grown in this

66
Three genii cucullati, *once interpreted as fertility goddesses but now thought to be minor local 'hooded spirits', each wearing the native* birrus Britannicus *hooded cloak.*

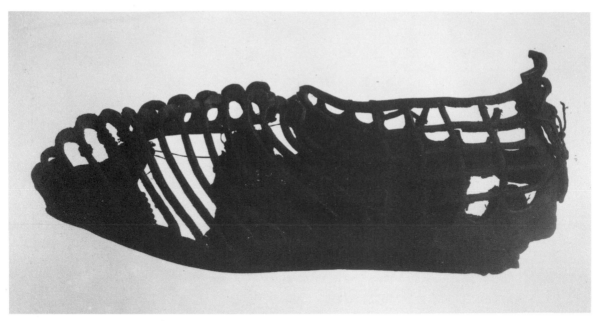

67
A leather openwork shoe.

country until within living memory: one of the last production plants was that near Wisbech, in Cambridgeshire, which closed down earlier this century. To produce the dye, the leaves were fermented and then dried on frames in the sun, after which they were heaped together for a second – and extremely noxious – fermentation, ultimately producing a ground powder. Madder roots were dried and ground also into powder.

Fullers not only dealt with new cloth, removing oil and grease with fuller's earth or bleaching it with infusions of sulphur, but also washed, dried and brushed garments handed in for cleaning by the city gentry.

Sandals and, for the ladies, slippers would be worn indoors; but out on the farm or going about their workaday tasks men would probably use the heavy leather shoes studded with nails of which many well-preserved examples and fragments have shown up in excavations.

All these necessities and luxuries had to be paid for. Primitive people had exchanged their own wares for others by systems of barter which were too untidy to work smoothly in a corporate state of the Roman pattern – and far too vague to assess properly for tax purposes, always a primary Roman consideration. Even before the Belgae reached Britain the inhabitants had for some time been using iron bars as a more manageable means of exchange. But far more convenient than such unwieldy currency was the introduction of coinage, copied by the Belgae from Greek models and introduced by them into their new territories. Gold was the favoured metal, though some coins were made of silver or bronze. After Caesar's brief incursion into south-eastern Britain there was not only an increase in trade between Rome and Britain, in spite of tribal dissensions, but a great spread of the use of gold and silver currency.

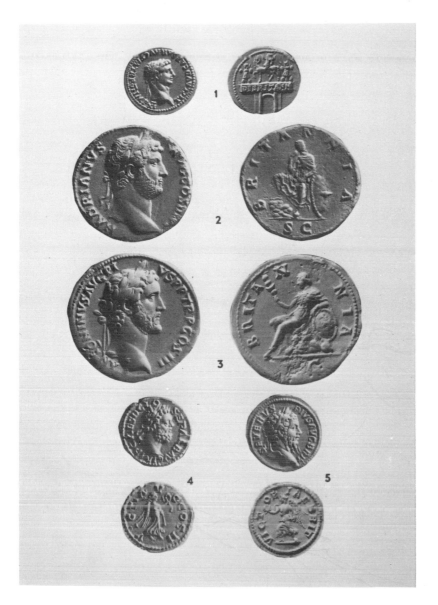

These coins were not merely tokens of exchange. The Romans and, in due course, their imitators used them for propaganda and celebratory purposes, featuring commemorative or informative pictures rather like those on our special issues of postage stamps, and of course imprinting the features and importance of local chieftains or the current Emperor on the minds of their subjects. To our own eyes there is something familiar in certain issues: the regal head on the obverse and the picture of Britannia on the reverse have been imitated with only a few lapses up to our own time.

For much of imperial history the standard Roman coin was the golden *denarius*. During the three centuries after Augustus had decreed its value,

68
Coins of Roman Britain, including examples with the archetypal Britannia on the reverse. The heads are those of (1) Claudius; (2) Hadrian; (3) Antonius Pius; (4) Clodius Albinus; (5) Septimius Severus.

there was a gradual devaluation until in the fourth century Constantine ordered the striking of a new denomination, the gold *solidus*. There were also several silver coins in general use, suffering similar debasement in due course by the introduction of increasing proportions of copper.

The original mints for supplying Britain were in Gaul, but even in the early years of occupation permission must have been given for copies to be issued from British sources: samples of silver *denarii*, probably rushed off the presses to pay the army, have been found at Fishbourne. When Gaul was caught up in the squabbles between rival contenders for the imperial throne – each circulating his image on rival coinage, though not for long in view of the shortness of his reign or campaign – Britain was left largely to herself for periods during which she had to produce her own money. London was the centre of this, though from time to time the mint there was closed down and then, in times of renewed stress, spasmodically reopened. Mint marks show the various places of origin: R, RM and ROM identify Rome; TR or TRE for Trier; L, LN and LON for London – and also AVG, dating coins to that period from the middle of the fourth century when London was known as Augusta.

When today we read gloomily in our newspapers or are lectured by professionally pessimistic faces on the television screen about our worsening exchange rates and the decline of the pound in our pocket, we may draw some consolation from the fact that we are by no means the first to suffer. When the Roman Empire declined, one of the first symptoms was the debasement of its coinage. On country estates and in the city market-places there must have been many who discovered that bartering real, solid goods and food was once again a more satisfactory arrangement than juggling with metal tokens.

CHAPTER V

DISTRIBUTION OF SITES

It has been remarked by many investigators that there are few traces of well-appointed houses on the villa pattern near such industrial sites as the Romans established. We have no obvious Romano–British equivalent of Josiah Wedgwood's home in the heart of his 'Etruria' enterprise in the Potteries, nor the splendid ironmasters' houses of the Sussex Weald; nor even, so far as we have yet discovered, of the flamboyant mansions built by Victorian tycoons on the ridges above that smoke and clangour which made their self-glorification possible.

Adhering to the strictest interpretation of the word 'villa' as meaning a farm and its associated buildings, it is of course hardly surprising that there should be no such estates linked with non-rural enterprises such as iron workings and furnaces, tin or lead mines, and stone quarries. Yet some semi-domestic processes such as weaving and the manufacture of pottery would surely have developed from individual villas in the first place before attaining factory output proportions; and even where we find no villa in the sense of a purely agricultural estate, if we allow ourselves to adopt a meaning slightly closer to our own usage could there really have been *no* house of any consequence for the supervisor of, say, a state weaving, fulling and dyeing works?

It may be that hitherto undiscovered villas existed in the industrial areas of those days. Nineteenth-century contractors were not as scrupulous or as interested in conservation as many of our contemporaries, and it is all too probable that any ancient remains which got in the way of new mill or foundry foundations, or hastily erected terraces for factory hands, would have been smashed through without delay. But just as a farmer in 1881 came across the first intimation of the long-forgotten Bignor villa when his plough struck a stone covering part of the dancers' mosaic, and a workman cutting a drainage trench in 1960 stumbled upon the palace at Fishbourne, so in this next decade or some decade in the farther future we may still hope to find, when digging drains for a new housing project or erecting a multi-storey car park, remains of the home of a chairman of some Romano–British nationalised industry, or the lessee of a lead mine. There must, after all, have been some perks and privileges for the men charged with enforcing maximum efficiency and output on workers in the localised crafts drawn together by Roman rationalisation.

Pottery making had ceased to be a cottage industry. Hand-made pots and bowls fired in rudimentary ovens or even in open fires had given way to the more consistent production of wares on potters' wheels, fired in more accurately controlled kilns. Whole settlements were devoted to this manufacture, the workshops being accompanied by living accommodation for the operatives – villages rather than villas. In the New Forest, a recognisable school in the late third and fourth centuries produced a greyish ware with brown or purplish glaze, and a creamier style with red decorative slip, sometimes with painted or stamped designs. There were fewer settlements in the Forest of Dean, where potters still practised on an itinerant, semi-nomadic basis, using the clay deposits and charcoal of one area until both clay and timber were exhausted, and then moving on in search of fresh supplies. More stable were the Castor-ware potteries along the Nene valley near Peterborough, where the owners or managers did in fact live in housing which might not be villas in the most academic sense, but were somewhat on the lines of our own conception of a comfortable bungalow.

69
Stone roof tiles from Wroxeter.

Similarly there were communities concentrating on tile making, iron working, and pewter. Distribution of the finished product presented no great problem: the roads which carried building materials such as Bath stone, Purbeck marble, regional specialities in slates and tiles, and foreign marble imported via warehouses in Colchester, could equally well transport finished goods of every description to towns, garrisons and seaports.

In Kent, where the fringes of Watling Street and the river valleys of the Medway, Darent and Stour bore the largest concentration of small estate villas so far uncovered, there were also concentrations of pottery kilns, tile and brick manufactories. One Kentish villa has yielded up what seems to be large fulling and dyeing tanks, and certainly there was a flourishing wool industry around Darenth. Stone was quarried near Lympne and near Maidstone, and tiles and bricks were made at Plaxtol. There were salt pans along the coast, and furnaces within or along the perimeters of the iron-bearing, timber-fuelling forests of the south-east.

The Romano–British iron industry was conceivably at its busiest around Battle and Crowhurst, and seems to have penetrated deeper into the Weald than was once supposed: cinder heaps with coins of Nero and Vespasian have been found in what must then have been thick woodland. Most of the extraction and smelting was carried out, however, in what Caesar referred to as '*in maritimus partibus*', and indeed may have been under the direct control of the Roman fleet – locally made tiles have been found stamped with the letters CL, BR, the *Classis Britannica* – or under that of local entrepreneurs working on contract to the fleet.

There is an impressive site near Wadhurst, along one bank of the little river Limden in East Sussex, where open-cast mining fed a second century group of smelting furnaces. By the beginning of the next century the buildings were converted into accommodation for the workers, and new shafts and furnaces established on smaller sites near by. Perhaps the wind changed unexpectedly one day and blew sparks and hot ash in the wrong direction, for there are indications that the main settlement was burnt down at one stage; but it was soon reconstructed, and digging and smelting continued, the furnaces being fed by plentiful supplies of charcoal from the woods of what the Romans knew as *Silva Anderida*.

What may have been the largest ironworks in the whole of Roman Britain was found a few years ago during work on a new housing estate at Broadfield, near Crawley. The building contractor and local authority proved generously cooperative, and the local archaeological society was given the opportunity of excavating and recording many details of the site. With two good surface veins of ore, it had obviously been in use before the Romans came, and they expanded it to a battery of over thirty furnaces, each about two feet wide. Most of the resulting pig iron was despatched to London. There are indications not merely of a workers' settlement here but also of a small military garrison, perhaps to supervise the workers or simply to establish and safeguard the imperial monopoly in minerals.

Two fairly lavish villas in north Lincolnshire, those at Winterton and Roxby, are not far from the Thealby iron workings of late Romano–British times, and could well have been the residences of government overseers or of private businessmen with concessions from the government. Winterton, in some respects suggesting a village rather than a self-contained villa, may have been supervised by one of the former, and settled by *coloni*; and there is evidence that it also supported its own weaving establishment.

A third Lincolnshire villa, that at Horkstow, yielded up a pavement with a racing scene which, viewed in conjunction with the estate's ideal meadowland setting, points to the possibility of its owner having specialised in breeding horses.

*   *   *

The use of enduring masonry was very restricted in some outlying regions. In East Anglia, where villa remains are sparse, it would appear that the majority rarely developed beyond the most simple timber framing upon foundations made from local flint. In the Fens, little exploited until the Romans made the first of many historic attempts to control the waters for irrigation and transport by digging canals and linking streams and rivers, local material such as clay, reeds and even turf were used – not by any means the usual Roman-inspired procedure. Later, as the region progressed, stone was brought in to strengthen or completely reconstruct a few of the more important buildings.

Smallholdings were run by farmers who often formed themselves, or were formed by government policy, into cooperative groups. Quite apart from increased efficiency of working and distribution, this made the assessment and collection of taxes easier. *Conductores*, licensed by the regional procurator, collected dues and percentages of produce, and were not above using their power and their knowledge of local conditions to make sly extra profits and collect bribes on the side. It was the activities of such middlemen which Agricola, early in the Roman occupation, had sought to regularise; but one cannot believe that they did not, then and later, find ways round inconvenient official injuctions.

Most of the buildings in such settings were conceived as straightforward farmhouses with plain living quarters, and remained as such until the decline of Roman military defences in this island, and loss of communication with the cities, forced them to concentrate on an even more spartan economy. Then the living rooms were converted into improvised workshops or storerooms, even their tessellated flooring being brutally mangled to accommodate corn-drying ovens and other immediate necessities. Iron workings impinged on the later phase of the Sutton Courtenay villa in Berkshire, and at one stage part of the temporarily abandoned Lullingstone house in Kent served as a tannery.

Traces of extensive villa estates any great distance from the favoured south and south-east have been few: a handful in the Welsh Marches, two on the coast beyond Cardiff, dangerously exposed to Irish raiders; and among those to the east of the Pennines, one bold venture which managed to run to the luxury of a bath-house in the far from hospitable military zone around Old Durham.

Soon after the Claudian conquest, fortifications were set up on Ermine Street at Great Casterton, in Rutland, from which an extensive town had developed by the late second century and which continued to grow within a loop of the river Gwash. Towards the end of the third century some influential citizen of the town built himself a large aisled barn about a quarter of a mile from the main fort. Originally there seem to have been no residential quarters, so the owner must have continued to live in the town and work his estate from there, perhaps accommodating some regular staff in the barn. As well as the timber-framed barn itself there were two other buildings, one of them probably a cart shed, the other a wide circular drying floor which may have been sheltered by a conical roof, the floor itself being heated through sunken ducts radiating from the centre like the spokes of a wheel. In the middle of the fourth century the existing buildings were demolished so that a full-scale house could be built on the site. This was added to during the next half century, until fire devastated the whole place. No attempt was made to restore the house itself, but some parts went on being used for storage, and a corn-drying oven was set up in the ruins. Doubtless the owner at that time wrote off the premises and stayed once more within the town; and the farm labourers would also find it wiser, in those troubled times of the early fifth century, to retreat within the town walls before darkness fell.

The only region to challenge the south-east in the proliferation of its villa estates is that around Bath. As well as being a spa for the treatment of ailing

70
The great Roman bath at Aquae Sulis (Bath).

71
A gilt-bronze head, presumed to be that of Minerva, found in Bath in 1727.

soldiers and civilians, the city became one of the main tourist centres for legionaries on leave, retired veterans, convalescents, and visitors from Rome itself. Such travellers must have felt comfortably at home among the fine streets and buildings of Aquae Sulis with its sumptuous baths, forum, statues, and temple dedicated to Sulis-Minerva. It was only to be expected that the well-to-do magistrates and dealers of such a prosperous city should acquire villas along the river and, indeed, out in all directions across the countryside within a radius of fifteen or sixteen miles. One house may have been the home of a quarry supervisor; another of a retired *decurion*; another of an inspector of the Mendip mines. Pewter was manufactured in the

neighbourhood, and here again a managerial salary or a merchant's profits may have contributed towards the comforts of a riverside villa.

On the Welsh littoral of the Bristol Channel about halfway between Barry and Porthcawl was the finely situated house of Llantwit Major, with superb vistas. But it was no holiday home. In one of the military zones of Wales, it carried on as a working farm with its own complex of workshops – all girdled by a ditch and earthen ramparts which protected the livestock against wild animals but could also serve as a defence against human marauders in an always uncertain region. The dwelling house and its farm buildings exemplify the intelligent use of local materials: limestone and

*72
A mask of Bath stone combining Celtic and Roman deities into Sulis-Minerva, masculine in appearance but deriving from the daughter of a water god and the Gorgon Medusa under the aegis of Minerva.*

sandstone, with a leavening of Bath stone shipped across the Bristol Channel. There were glazed windows, a bath suite, and mosaic pavements. By the end of the third century, though, this agreeable dwelling had been burnt down and was apparently abandoned by its owner, who relinquished the accompanying barn to his bailiff, labourers and slaves.

Even where men of humbler standing worked in town or village communities with no grandiose aspirations towards acquiring their own country estates, their livelihood might critically depend on the prosperity of the landlords and the very existence of those villas. The schools of mosaicists which had sprung up throughout the country found plenty of regular work in fashionable quarters of the towns; but plenty, also, in villas of the neighbourhood. From copying Continental models they progressed to the compilation of their own pattern books, which they would show to prospective customers, quoting a standard price per square foot for simple borders and repetitive geometric patterns (doubtless with some addition for travelling time, increasing cost of raw materials, government taxation, and so on) and offering to incorporate special motifs on request for an agreed extra sum. There is a marked similarity between pavements at Fishbourne and those at Angmering some twelve miles along the coast: it could well be that after completion of a major commission the workshop would seek similar employment in the district.

Other bodies of artisans supplied complementary needs: tiles and paving stones, ceramic or lead water pipes, lamps, metalwork, specialised joinery, and sculpted masonry.

To see surviving examples of these contributions in their proper context, one needs to select the most thoroughly excavated and documented remaining villas preserved in private hands or under the auspices of the National Trust or Department of the Environment. Over 600 have been located, and of these some ten per cent are lavishly appointed and, where accessible, worthy of sustained examination. There are traces of lesser importance on various sites, meriting a visit if one is in the district but revelatory only to those who have some visual recollection of the layout of richer remains.

*   *   *

Two ruins on the cliff above East Wear Bay, Folkestone, can be easily reached but have less and less to show as the years go by: if there are any further cliff subsidences, one of them is likely to disappear completely. In the same county, Kent, Otford revealed some wall plaster painted with scenes and quotations from Vergil. Just over the Surrey border from Kent are preserved the footings of a villa excavated at Titsey in the last century, overgrown but demarcating its original outlines.

73
A re-creation of Lullingstone villa, Kent, by Alan Sorrell.

A little way to the north-east of Titsey is the extensive villa of Lullingstone in the Darent valley. This came to the surface again 200 years ago when posts for a deer fence were driven through a section of mosaic flooring representing the Seasons. The head of Summer was badly mutilated, and Winter suffered some damage also from these stakes, but apart from recording the existence of the mosaic no great concern was shown at the time. It was not until 1949 that scrupulous excavation began, and gradually the true proportions of the buried buildings were disclosed.

There had once been a massive granary with flint and mortar walls, covered by a thatched roof. Its drying hall had 28 piers to support the wooden floor, and there was a narrower aisle along the southern edge with a red-tiled roof. Towards the end of the fourth century this building had degenerated into a cart shed and chicken run, and in due course most of the building was demolished. The twentieth-century archaeologists carefully analysed its basic layout and then, to protect it from the elements, filled it in again.

In the northern section of the complex is a 'deep room' whose wall paintings intimate that there must once have been an important spring here. Worship of the attendant spirit was counter-balanced by the construction of a Christian chapel.

74
Mosaic of Europa and the bull from Lullingstone, accompanied by playful Cupids. The couplet above is a comment on a passage in the first book of Vergil's Aeneid.

Mosaics include a fine one of Europa and the bull; Bellerophon upon Pegasus slaying the Chimera; and three surviving elements of the Four Seasons. Second-century marble busts, a unique find in Britain, seem to represent noble Romans rather than Romano–Britons and may be survivals of an ancestral portrait gallery: the originals are to be found in the British Museum, but replicas are displayed on the site.

Other finds, here as elsewhere, are in their way more touching because of the more vivid personal contact they establish: such everyday trivia as pins, needles, brooches and rings. There are also the bones of many animals; and of three small children.

In Sussex is Bignor villa, mentioned earlier. Standing close to the old line of Stane Street north-east of Chichester, it can be shown to have started life as a simple timber-framed house which was burnt down and replaced by an equally simple stone cottage. Gradually it expanded into a courtyard house with between 50 and 60 rooms, of which six are now preserved with their remarkable mosaics in huts with thatched roofs which, from a distance, give the place the incongruous appearance of a native kraal. The villa had central heating, coloured wall plaster decorations and a complicated water supply which must have been pumped from a stream over the crest of a low hill to the north of the house and then allowed to run downhill of its own accord to the farmyard and its buildings. Among the mosaics are one of the beautiful young Ganymede being kidnapped by an eagle to serve as Jupiter's cup-bearer; a rectangle of geometric patterns framing a vase of flowers; and the head and shoulders of a wistful, meditative Venus accompanied by flowers and pheasants, with a panel of gladiators attired as winged Cupids. A feature of this haloed Venus is the unusual smallness of the stone cubes in the mosaic, giving a much more delicate effect than one finds in the larger inlays.

Various owners of Bignor may have been connected with the city of Chichester and its harbour at Fishbourne. Though a royal palace rather than a villa, Fishbourne merits a visit because so many of its constructional and decorative features parallel those of otherwise submerged and probably irreclaimable villas: the mosaics, the well-appointed bath suite, fragments

75
Marble portrait bust from Lullingstone of what appears to be a member of the family living here, probably carved by an immigrant sculptor in the Roman rather than the adapted Romano–British tradition.

of painted wall plaster, decorative friezes in moulded stucco, and the conjecturally restored gardens. The museum displays a wide range of small objects and fragments found during excavation, any one of which would have been equally at home on one of the country estates.

The rediscovery of Chedworth villa in Gloucestershire was, like that of Bignor, Fishbourne and Lullingstone, the result of a happy accident. In 1864 it was literally reopened to the world by a gamekeeper trying to dig out his ferret. The first building arose in the second century, but the remains we can see now were those of the fourth century, abandoned after a few decades of residence. The spring supplying the large stone water basins and the two bath suites has never been known to run dry, and continues to supply water to the modern house. Footings of buildings surrounding a main courtyard have been cleared, along with one wing of the villa, and roofed over where the mosaic floors need protection. In its time it must have been one of the most comfortable and gracious homes in the land, and in its wooded setting is still surely the most attractive and evocative of all villa sites.

In the same county is Woodchester, its villa infringing on the churchyard. This, one of the most extensive courtyard villas in the country, has the largest mosaic so far unearthed in Britain. Some 50 feet square, it depicts Orpheus within concentric circles of birds and animals, watched over by water nymphs, within a frame of geometric panels which give the whole thing the appearance of an Eastern carpet. The floor required about $1\frac{1}{2}$ million cubes, installed by the Cirencester workshop which seems also to have been responsible for the mosaics at Chedworth. It is displayed only rarely to the public, and the earnest pilgrim will need to keep an eye open for announcements of such unveilings.

Though less impressive, some remains of Witcombe villa, another of the Cotswold group, are more easily and frequently accessible. Exposure to weather since the first discoveries in 1818 has, however, unfortunately resulted in the fading of the original coloured wall panels; but fragments of plaster with attractive flower and leaf patterns have been found and, in recent times, more carefully preserved.

Some unusual mosaics representing the Eleusinian mysteries are to be found in the villa at Brading, Isle of Wight, a fourth-century house of the winged corridor type adjoining a large square courtyard flanked by other buildings. This is one of those houses encroached on in its declining years by crude materialism – or the demands of sheer survival – when a furnace was set into one of its mosaic floors.

Even more markedly utilitarian is the site at Hambleden in Buckinghamshire. The plan on p. 35 shows the busy cluster of buildings around the farmyard, and excavation has shown these to have been filled with corn-drying kilns, flour mills, and all the other equipment of a hard-working agricultural enterprise. It has been suggested that this was no private estate but an official collection, processing and distribution point for corn. Most of the tasks were probably carried out by slave labour: it was beside these buildings that such a significant concentration of infant burials was found.

Rather more civilised is the house at Ditchley, north of Woodstock in Oxfordshire, where a simple basic farmhouse acquired large private rooms at each end and, having at first been accompanied by a barn with the usual equipment and living quarters for the staff, eventually replaced this with a large granary. At the same time, the main house was further expanded. The change might indicate that the owner himself had moved away to the city, allowing his bailiff and family to lodge in the more comfortable quarters. Although there may originally have been slaves on the estate, its later phases show no sign of accommodation for them.

By the third and fourth centuries even the Brigantes, profiting more from peaceful trade with the Romans and their Romanised neighbours than from fruitless quarrels with them, had grudgingly accepted many of the Roman appurtenances which went with such prosperity. There might still be cave dwellers in Yorkshire and, of course, the Derbyshire Peak District; but many had turned away from the nomadic life. The quality of the villa of Stancil, south of Doncaster, with its third-century bath-house, and the existence of two other substantial villas in the neighbourhood, shows that settled and productive farming was no longer scorned by the men of the north and the uplands.

Aldborough in Yorkshire, which as Isurium Brigantum became the Romanised capital of the Brigantes, was a considerable township and therefore, strictly speaking, outside our terms of reference. But it would be a pity

76
The legend of Rome's founding twins, Romulus and Remus, under the care of their foster-mother wolf, as interpreted in a mosaic in the Brigantian capital at Aldborough though the distorted animal seems inadequately endowed for suckling the two skittish infants.

to omit all mention of it, since within the confines of this tribal headquarters are many indications of the way in which Roman influences had reached out into once unreceptive regions. The extent of the community can be gauged by the scattered remnants which have shown up within the present village at one time and another: a mosaic pavement sheltered from the weather within a private house, another at the back of the local pub, and walls and ramparts of the original town showing up behind the little museum and along a patch of allotments. The remains of a house which obviously belonged to a man of consequence had much in common with a villa house, including fine wall plaster depicting the Muses, accompanied by an inscription in Greek. Comparison with plaster fragments and patterns from villa estates in the region suggests that Aldborough was in fact the centre of a flourishing school of painters and decorators, serving the needs of landowners over quite a wide area.

To track down and fully appreciate the most rewarding villa sites, one should first study the Ordnance Survey map of Roman Britain; and then set out with a reliable guidebook such as R.J.A. Wilson's 'Roman Remains in Britain', which achieves a remarkable feat of compression without ever seeming too brief or perfunctory.

77
The goddess Brigantia represented in stone at Blatobulgium (Birrens, Dumfriesshire). In the third century attempts were made to raise this local deity to the status of a major cult figure with Roman-inspired trappings such as Minerva's spear and shield, and the wings of Victory, but still wearing a native helmet and crown to indicate her British regality.

CHAPTER VI

DECLINE OF THE VILLA

In his play 'The Long Sunset', R.C. Sheriff conjures up a picture of the last stages of Roman occupation in the fifth century – that 'age of crépuscule and quicksand', as Sir Mortimer Wheeler once put it. The scene is set in a villa near Richborough, overlooking the once proud port through which the last legionaries are departing. The main characters are slightly implausible in that they are, after all these centuries, of pure Roman stock. By this period of history the bulk of the legions had already gone and it seems unlikely that any patrician Roman would still be clinging to an estate in such a region, trying to make a success of subsistence farming, or that any man would speak as Marcus does to his friend Julian of the scant cooperation they may expect in this crisis from the native Britons: 'We came here as conquerors four hundred years ago and we've remained as conquerors ever since.' Though a number of inevitable dissidents had resented Roman hegemony, just as they would have resented the presence of any other powerful ruler, the majority – and especially those in the south-east – had learned the advantages of cooperation, and both spoke and thought in Roman terms.

A rough mercenary appears on the scene: one Arthur, an uncouth but invigorating character who offers the only hope of uniting scattered patriotic forces and putting up some resistance to the aggressors who, having reduced the Continental provinces to chaos, are now turning their full attention to the island of Britain. There are many over-simplifications in his attitude, as in those of the Romans, and a sentimental ending when the villa owner and his wife finally decide they must go, leaving behind only a glimmer of light on the Christian altar, symbolic of the light which after years of oncoming darkness will eventually be rekindled; but whatever errors of fact or judgment there may be at certain moments in the play, the whole piece is atmospheric and wonderfully evocative, conveying the sad, dying cadences of a collapsing civilisation.

The ending did not in fact come quite so suddenly and dramatically. No educated man could have been as unaware as the bewildered Julian is of the true state of affairs. There was no abrupt scurrying of the legions from these shores, and no all-out attack by an organised enemy as with the Claudian invasion and later, even more purposefully, the invasion by William the Conqueror. The rot set in gradually, over a couple of centuries: the slow crumbling of decay rather than the immediate impact of a mass bombing raid.

It had never been possible to complete the subduing of the extreme north, and even Agricola was forced to leave the situation there in a state of flux. By the time Hadrian became Emperor in AD 117, Agricola's few remaining achievements in that direction had had to be abandoned. Hadrian himself was far from wishing to initiate any punitive campaigns: he had already decided that, to avoid over-stretching Rome's military resources, Assyria, Mesopotamia and other imperial eastern annexations must be discarded. But when serious rebellions broke out in Britain during the time when he was making the sort of grand self-advertising tour which in a later century Queen Elizabeth I, for example, found it expedient to make, he decided the time had come for a grand gesture. Deciding to abandon the entire territory north of the Tyne gap and so save manpower, but at the same time to ensure that no major assaults could be launched from that territory, in 122 he decreed the building of a wall over seventy miles long across the vulnerable neck of Britain between Bowness on the Solway firth to Wallsend on the north bank of the river Tyne. Forts known as milecastles were erected at intervals of a Roman mile (about ten per cent longer than our own mile), garrisoned not by regular legionaries but by lesser cohorts from Iberian and North African provinces, together with a few Britons. Between the milecastles were watch-towers, and at wider intervals were fortresses with substantial garrisons and supply dumps.

This vast building project took about ten years to complete, and very soon after that completion a number of the troops estimated as necessary for its protection were withdrawn to deal with revolts in other parts of the Empire. The thinned-out defence forces were exposed to renewed attack from opportunists along their own new frontier. Antonius Pius ordered that a further wall – this time merely an earthen rampart – should be set up between the Clyde and the Forth, to establish another obstacle in the path of those planning to rampage down into lowland Britain, which had always been Rome's main concern.

Danger came, however, not merely from enemies beyond the Antonine Wall. From time to time there were uprisings of dissatisfied tribes, especially in highland regions, who had never felt altogether at peace with the *pax Romana*. When the Emperor Commodus was assassinated in 192, three contenders strove for the throne. One of these was Clodius Albinus, governor of Britain, who set himself at the head of most of the Roman army in the province and took it away with him into Gaul. His campaign failed and he committed suicide. In the absence of the army, tribes from beyond the two ill-manned walls broke through and devastated northern Britain.

The new Emperor, Septimius Severus, issued instructions for a massive rebuilding of Hadrian's Wall and came personally to the province to force back invaders and quell internal revolts.

After this the third century was one of relative calm and prosperity for Britain, though not for the rest of the Empire. Twenty-five Emperors came to power within a space of 50 years, usually achieving their goal by treachery and the suborning of troops under their immediate command. When successful, they could look forward to being assassinated within a year or two. The breakdown of a united imperial army and the civil administration into rival factions, susceptible to bribery and flamboyant promises, made it easy for barbarian raiders to strike across the Roman frontiers. Sometimes the intruders killed and looted in hit-and-run style; at other times, large war bands ravaged town and countryside.

Continental villa owners fled to the towns or, in some cases, to Britain, leaving their houses to be burnt down by invaders or by careless squatters.

Towards the end of the century Britain began to feel the resonance of these disturbances, though at first only in everyday economic terms. The coinage began to slide into what ultimately became an inflationary degeneration. Imports from the strife-torn areas dried up. Taxes were increased to pay for defence of far colonies, when the defence of Britain itself was demonstrably inadequate. Some villas were abandoned, others deteriorated from lack of maintenance.

When Saxon pirates began to turn their attention to Britain and particularly to the rich pickings of the south-eastern region, many owners deemed it prudent to stay in their town houses within strong fortifications, leaving an agent in the country villa to supervise those peasants who could not afford to seek employment elsewhere but who, equally, had no taste for redecorating or even keeping in good condition the originally luxurious trappings of the homestead. Workers and slaves who did flee the premises did so in order to turn brigand, in emulation of the Saxons who were harrying the land.

In the 280's a Belgic seaman in Roman service, Carausius, was given the task of clearing the North Sea and English channel of such pirates. He more than anyone else was responsible for the creation or reinforcement of the forts of 'the Saxon Shore' between the Wash and Hampshire. But his achievements in this theatre of operations were designed as much for his own ultimate advancement as for the fulfilment of his official commission. Rumours spread that he was in league with certain groups of pirates and that between them they had devised a system of sharing out booty before he made a token arrest of some hapless scapegoat.

Before he could be relieved of his command and brought to justice, Carausius bought the loyalty of the British legions with his ill-gotten gains, proclaimed himself regional Emperor, and for six years held on to Britain and a considerable part of Gaul. Coinage was struck showing his head on a level with those other two Emperors who at the time were sharing out other

78
*Coins of (1) Carausius,
admiral of the Classis
Britannica, and Emperor
c. AD 287, and (2) Allectus,
his finance minister who turned
traitor to assassinate and
supersede him.*

Roman territories between them. Declaring himself *Restitutor Britanniae*, the Restorer of Britain, Carausius continued strengthening the forts along the coast, this time to protect himself against the masters who had hired him.

Yet this was a time of extension and elaboration of many of the richer country villas. Perhaps their owners had grown optimistic again. A firm hand was needed, and they thought Carausius was the man to apply it. The time was ripe for a local patriot who would stand no nonsense. Some folk have always had a longing for that unlikeliest of all beings, a benevolent dictator. In times of trouble the Romans had been prone to ignore this outpost of Empire. A local chauvinist leader, however self-seeking, might be no bad thing. So long as the still uncoordinated barbarians could be held at bay by such a disciplinarian, the taxpayers could continue their civilised way of life. And if the worst came to the worst, it was still possible to command a high price for one's property from one of the many refugees from Gaul who still regarded Britain as the safest of all available havens in an unsteady world.

In 293 Carausius was assassinated by one of his ministers, Allectus, who thereafter enjoyed only a brief reign. Threatened with imperial reconquest by legions under Constantius Chlorus, he desperately assembled an army from the northern garrisons, with the inevitable result: Picts came swarming once again over Hadrian's Wall, this time penetrating as far south as York and Chester. Constantius' first task after defeating Allectus was to rebuild that battle-scarred frontier.

All this, together with the cost of holding at bay pinprick sallies by Saxon marauders, meant an increase in the taxes and social duties of the more prosperous townsfolk. Fortifications had to be strengthened, there was an increase in the size and activity of naval patrols; yet each time additional dues had been levied for building up a worthier army, that army was depleted by urgent demands from faraway imperial battlegrounds. Where necessary, private property was sold, and some private estates were commandeered.

Still no really large-scale attack threatened until well into the next century.

In 367 the Picts, Scots and Saxons joined forces. Forts and milecastles of Hadrian's Wall succumbed yet again. Deserters from scattered army units and minor garrisons threw in their lot with the invaders. Forces under the commander of the province were cut off before they could retaliate; and the Count of the Saxon Shore was killed. Defences everywhere were in a shambles. The Emperor sent Count Theodosius to restore order, which he did with such vigour that at last there were signs of a rebirth of that prosperity which Romanised Britain had earlier enjoyed. Further fortification of town and city walls gave craftsmen, merchants and the local nobility renewed confidence. All might yet go well.

The slow decline of the villas at the end of the third century and early in the fourth was arrested. Standing to some extent aloof from Continental disturbances, apart from times when their own troops were called upon, the Romano–Britons might regard with some complacency the strife which, with a bit of luck, would keep both their Roman overlords and their barbarian enemies busy. They began to put their recently neglected homesteads to rights. Old villas were refurbished and extended. New villas sprang up on new sites, more elaborate than ever before. One factor which encouraged this return to the countryside was the continuing increase in urban taxes and responsibilities mentioned above. Those of the city dignitaries who could manage to do so discarded their civic duties and went to live permanently on their rural estates.

79
Hadrian's wall: a corner of the fortress at Vercovicium (Housesteads), where ramparts, barracks and granaries have all been well preserved, and whose museum contains some of the most evocative finds made in the region.

Potteries in Gaul were destroyed; so native potters moved vigorously into the market. Weavers intensified their local efforts. Resident landowners farmed their lands more intensively. The country could surely be made self-sufficient. 'Dig for Victory' and 'Buy British' might well have been the slogans. And this, too, was the period of the finest, most sophisticated mosaics.

*   *   *

Life in the country may have been just a bit too escapist. The villa owner who turned his back on the town was in danger of missing the latest despatches and rumours, and probably shut his eyes and ears when he went briefly back on shopping trips to the urban streets – shut them to the increasing number of swaggering foreign mercenaries, to the breakdown of hitherto smooth-running services, and to the unease in people's faces and voices. The boisterous jokes in the public baths turned ugly and xenophobic; there was talk of U.D.I. – unilateral declaration of independence by Britain; and increasing personal frustrations brought increasing collective gloom.

For the calm did not last. In 383 Magnus Maximus, Roman military commander in Britain, dissatisfied with his own status and with the Emperor Gratian's dangerous favouritism towards German mercenaries, took a familiar course: setting his sights on becoming western Emperor, he drained British defences of troops so that he might lead them across Europe to pursue his personal campaign. At first he was successful. But there were now three contesting would-be Emperors, and Magnus Maximus did not dare to let his troops return to Britain: they were needed on the spot to defend his seizure of Gaul and Spain. After his death in battle against the eastern Emperor Theodosius, dissension continued within the Empire, and the ripples reaching British shores began to build up into storm waves.

By encouraging the transfer of Roman rule in the north to a number of petty kingdoms, one of them extending as far south as York, and by hiring German mercenaries to make up for deficiencies in Romano–British defences, Count Theodosius had laid up trouble for his successors. Devolution of imperial power led inevitably to civil and military fragmentation. Withdrawal of increasing numbers of Roman functionaries to cope with urgent problems elsewhere had, over a long period, meant the transfer of regional administration into the hands of British magistrates and councillors; but at their gates, greedy and watchful, were the cousins of those very barbarians who at this moment were carving the Empire apart.

In 395, when the boy Honorius became Emperor, Britain had no organised defence system worth speaking of. The legions had dwindled. Civilian experts had gone. Irish invaders established themselves in Wales. In spite of treaties and compromises, the north was in renewed ferment. Appeals for the supply of more trained soldiers brought one moderately successful expedition under the command of a general who was himself a Vandal. Further pleas went unheeded.

In 407 another would-be autarch – 'Britain is a land fertile in usurpers', commented the historian monk, Gildas – achieved nothing within the country but further disruption. At about this same time the military commanders in Gaul appealed to Britain for aid, and now the Romano–British had to make a crucial decision: could Gaul and Britain triumph in partnership, or should Britain stand alone and, behind the barrier of the Channel, rely on a siege economy?

An attempted alliance fell through because of the misguided attempt of its commander to set himself up as Constantine III and take over Spain and parts of Italy itself. Britain must henceforth stand alone.

Thus further weakened, the province was now subjected to direct assault of the kind the Continental provinces had long been enduring. Disillusioned with Roman inadequacy, the towns followed the example of many of their counterparts in Gaul and announced that from now on all administration would be in British hands.

Perhaps they still, in spite of this bravado, did not quite believe the Romans were gone forever. Even while 'living on their own, no longer obedient to Roman laws', as the Greek historian Zosimus puts it, they must have half hoped for a firm restitution of the imperial verities – and comforts.

In 410 the Emperor Honorius sent a fateful message. Addressing local councils in the Britannic province, he exhorted them to see to their own defences, and formally rescinded that clause of the Julian Law which forbade civilians to bear arms without specific imperial permission.

Life went on in the towns and on the larger villa estates. Few even of those who sensed the rumblings of the eventual earthquake sought to flee the country: things were so much worse across the Channel and the North Sea that refugees were still arriving in large numbers in what they regarded as the last possible bastion against the barbarians.

But the barbarians themselves were also infiltrating. Unpredictable raids by Saxons and Picts could devastate farms, lead to pitched battles, and dissolve into far-ranging skirmishes in which one isolated villa might be razed to the ground while, in a neighbouring part of the country, another villa owner might blandly be commissioning a lavish new mosaic or mural. And, even more insidiously, enemies were actually being invited to immigrate and make themselves at home.

One of the regional potentates who sprang up in the wake of the Roman defection is generally referred to by the name of Vortigern, though scholars still disagree over his identity and even the likely dates of his reign. It is, however, Vortigern who has generally been blamed for inviting a growing number of Saxons into southern Britain, offering them land for settlement in return for their help against the persistently marauding Picts and Scots. Tradition has it that the two major chieftains with whom he dealt were

80
The mosaic of a misshapen Venus with a merman – apparently pursuing her with a back-scratcher – from the Rudston villa in Yorkshire, now in the Hull Museum. An example of shoddy, distorted work late in the Romano–British era by a local craftsman unskilled in the niceties of classical mosaics produced in the hey-day of the major regional workshops.

Hengist and Horsa. Once established, these warriors lost no time in quarrelling with their host and, now allying themselves with the very Picts against whom they had contracted to defend Britain, set about pillaging the entire countryside.

Only the most stubborn landowners still occupied their villas in that countryside. Even if they had cared to risk a sort of lawless Wild West existence in their frontier ranches, communications with the towns and with such armed neighbours as could be relied on were hopelessly disrupted by now. Maintenance of the road network required a military and civil engineering organisation which no longer existed. With no legion commanders to insist on their preservation, and no busy inter-city or import trade traffic such as there had once been, the surfaces cracked, the causeways sagged, and weed began to grow over the tumbled stones. Even before the Saxons prevailed and began to create their own crude pattern of paths and trackways, the despondent Britons had abandoned any attempt to maintain the roads and resorted to treading out paths in the earth beside the *agger*.

Cut off from towns and farming neighbours, few villas could, despite their best efforts, be entirely self-supporting and self-protecting. The Roman tradition which had dominated life, work and thought here for several hundred years was focused on the towns, and the Roman way of life depended on that relationship. Having for a while abandoned the towns for the villas, most owners now huddled back into the towns for what promised to be a last stand against the invaders. Their country properties were left to decay or, in the hands of some peasant farmer and his family, to suffer the indignity of being reduced to sheds and workrooms with, as we have already noted, ovens and other equipment clumsily inserted into tiled bath-houses or mosaic floors.

At Llantwit Major, there had been a time when the owner's residence and the aisled barn for staff and storage had formed a companionable unity. Towards the end, the residential quarters were abandoned, leaving the farm in the hands of the labourers who lived in the barn – for where else could they go?

A handful of villas survived in the hands of owners influential enough to be able to hire mercenaries to guard them. But, protected or unprotected, they were all at risk of attack by invaders or disaffected Britons – army deserters and runaway serfs.

When excavations reveal charred timbers and tiles, it is natural to assume that the villa concerned was burnt by raiders; but many may well have been destroyed or partially damaged by accident. There is no reason to suppose, for instance, that the burning of Lullingstone early in the fifth century was other than accidental. Here and there one does, however, come across irrefutable evidence of a savage raid. At King's Weston in Gloucestershire, where one wing was gutted by fire, the remains enshrine a skeleton with sword cuts in its skull. At North Wraxall in Wiltshire, corpses and fragments of Roman armour were found thrown with other débris to the bottom of a well.

Throughout the decades of decline, coinage throughout the Empire had been debased. Britain did not escape this demonetisation and inflation, despite internal attempts at one time and another to reform the currency. The sound gold *aureus* and silver *denarius* gave way to tiny, locally struck *minimissimi* and other denominations heavily mixed with baser metal. Yet, unstable as its value was, people still hoarded that money. And when the time came to flee, in whatever direction, they often buried it in the pathetic hope of coming back one happier day and retrieving it. Not far from Wiggonholt villa, Pulborough, almost 2000 late Roman coins were found packed neatly in wooden boxes. Near the Suffolk coast, a buried leaden box contained nearly 1000 silver coins. Other householders, fearful of robbers who would strip the house and scour the grounds for such valuables, seem to have taken their treasures well away from their homes and buried them in open fields or corners with which they, and only they, would be familiar. One such hoard was the superb collection of imported silver tableware unearthed by a ploughman near Mildenhall, Suffolk, in 1942.

81
In 1942 thirty-four pieces of heavily encrusted tableware were ploughed up near Mildenhall, Suffolk. At first thought to be pewter, they proved after cleaning to be silver, most probably made in the Eastern Empire. A large proportion of the designs have pagan themes, with a leaning towards Bacchic revelry; but also in the treasure are some spoons inscribed with the Chi-rho monogram, suggesting that the well-to-do family who buried it may towards the end have been practising Christians. Shown here are (left) a flanged bowl and lid, and (over) two platters with dancing maenads accompanied in one case by Pan and in the other by a satyr.

Craftsmen's tools have been found in wells at Silchester, Great Chester-
ford, and other places, suggesting hurried concealment from approaching
enemies, and that same hope of return one day.

At Water Newton was hidden the earliest known collection of Christian
plate, 300 years before the arrival of St Augustine on these shores, precious
even by purely monetary standards. It may have been buried during
Diocletian's persecution of Christians, and never reclaimed.

In the West Country, with Irish raiders striking from one direction and
the Saxons flowing remorselessly in from another, many Britons appear to
have forsaken the last vestiges of Roman buildings and Roman ways, and
fled as a last resort to their old tribal hill-top fortifications. They took with
them their Romanised money and household goods – on many sites,
especially in Wales, there have been substantial finds of coins and pottery –
but, Roman emperors and Roman gods having failed them, they sought the
forgiveness and aid of older gods. The revival of ancient pagan cults
ensured that religious schism accompanied the breakdown of social
customs. A new temple was built within the ramparts of Maiden Castle,
and there was one, possibly two, on Chanctonbury Ring.

The most extensive of these shrines, however, is that discovered by Sir
Mortimer Wheeler at Lydney on the Severn, between Gloucester and
Chepstow. It was built in honour of the Celtic deity Nodens, within a pre-
historic hill-top fort, and equipped with a guest-house, baths, and sleep and
meditation rooms for pilgrims. The cult of Nodens attracted many wealthy
folk: among the offerings found on the site were more than 8000 coins.
Roman-trained officers were not above offering their respects to this older
British god, as is shown by the dedication of a mosaic by a prefect from a
naval station on the Bristol Channel.

*   *   *

As for the abandoned villas, the Saxons showed little inclination to take
them over. Their chiefs preferred a social life in great wooden halls; the
poorer settlers passed a squalid and rheumaticky existence in hovels with
floors set two feet below ground level so that the crude roofs could rest on
the earth to either side – a reversion to the standards of 1000 or more years
earlier. Only here and there do we find cases of a villa site being occupied
by the new conquerors; and then it was probably the agricultural possibilities and the existence of a good water supply which lured them rather than
the existence of a ready-made homestead. At Litlington in Hertfordshire
there are signs of continuity from Celtic times through the years when a
villa and a Romano–British cemetery existed there, and on through Anglo-
Saxon occupation. Eynsham, on the Thames in Oxfordshire, was a village
whose Romanisation is attested by finds of coins from successive centuries
but whose very name speaks of later Saxon settlement. Ashmore, the highest

village in Dorset, is also Saxon – 'the mere of the ash tree' – but traces of old earthworks suggest an earlier hill-top fort, and all around it are other Romano–British villages.

But isolated survivors do not add up to a healthy, living tradition. The walls which had sheltered the Romano–British way of life became mere shells. A whole study course could be devoted to the analysis of soil movements and climatic changes which resulted in the disappearance of those remaining walls and foundations below ground and thus, for the pleasure of later generations, their preservation; but in the end it must be acknowledged that, like the burial of Pharaohs within sunken chambers or deep inside the Pyramids, it was indeed the burial of something which no longer had the vitality to maintain itself or the complex civilisation which had brought it into being.

82
All that remains of the north
wing at Chedworth.

SELECT BIBLIOGRAPHY

ALCOCK, LESLIE: *Arthur's Britain* (Allen Lane, 1971)

BIRLEY, ANTHONY: *Life in Roman Britain* (Batsford, 1964)

BLAIR, P. HUNTER: *Roman Britain and Early England* (Nelson, 1963)

BRAILSFORD, J.W.: *Guide to the Antiquities of Roman Britain* (British Museum, 3rd edn 1964)

COLLINGWOOD. R.G., AND RICHMOND, I.A.: *Archaeology of Roman Britain* (Methuen, 1969)

CORDER, PHILIP (ed): *The Roman Town and Villa at Great Casterton* (University of Nottingham reports, 1954–61)

COTTRELL, LEONARD: *Seeing Roman Britain* (Evans, 1956)

DIVINE, DAVID: *The North-West Frontier of Rome* (Macdonald, 1969)

FLEURE, H.J., AND DAVIES, M.: *A Natural History of Man in Britain* (Fontana, 1971)

FRERE, SHEPPARD: *Britannia* (Routledge & Kegan Paul, 1967)

HELM, P.J.: *Exploring Roman Britain* (Hale, 1975)

HOSKINS, W.G.: *The Making of the English Landscape* (Hodder & Stoughton, 1955)

MARGARY, I.D.: *Roman Ways in the Weald* (Phoenix House, 1948)

MEATES, G.W.: *Lullingstone Roman Villa* (Heinemann, 1955)

PERCIVAL, JOHN: *The Roman Villa* (Batsford, 1976)

QUENNELL, M. & C.H.B.: *Everyday Life in Roman Britain* (Batsford, 1924 – frequently reprinted and revised)

RAINEY, A.: *Mosaics in Roman Britain* (David & Charles, 1973)

RICHMOND, I.A.: *Roman Britain* (Penguin, 1955)

RICHMOND, I.A. (ed): *Roman and Native in North Britain* (Nelson, 1958)

RICHMOND, I.A.: *Roman Archaeology and Art* (Faber, 1969)

RIVET, A.L.F. (ed): *Town and Country in Roman Britain* (Hutchinson, 1958)

WHITE, K.D.: *Farm Equipment of the Roman World* (Cambridge University Press, 1967, reprinted 1975)

WHITWELL, J.B.: *Roman Lincolnshire* (Lincolnshire Local History Society, 1970)

WILSON, R.J.A.: *Roman Remains in Britain* (Constable, 1975)

INDEX